BUILDING
Bridges

A Wood Dragon Book

BUILDING
Bridges

A BIG CITY MAYOR
REFLECTS ON LEADERSHIP

Donald J. Atchison

A Wood Dragon Book

Building Bridges –
A Big City Mayor Reflects on Leadership

Copyright © 2025 by Donald J. Atchison

ISBN: 978-1-990863-84-4 Hardcover
ISBN: 978-1-990863-74-5 Paperback
ISBN: 978-1-990863-73-8 eBook

Cover Design: Callum Jagger, Hyperlight Artwork
Interior Design: Christine Lee

Published by: Wood Dragon Books
Post Office Box 429
Mossbank, Saskatchewan, Canada S0H3G0
www.wooddragonbooks.com

To contact the publisher: wooddragonbooks@gmail.com
To contact the author: d.atch@shaw.ca

For more information about the book:
https://linktr.ee/Don.Atchison

Contents

Dedication

To my wife Mardele (who has been my strength) and my children Carrie, Don Jr., Jason, Brielle, and Aria. I would not have been able to be the mayor without your constant support and encouragement for all those years. I thank each and every one of you for forgiving me for not being at every birthday party or staying for every event.

To my father Frank

Dad was christened Francis, a name that he said no one should say aloud. He was a visionary, yet was a cautious one, never wanting to set goals too lofty for fear of failure. There wasn't a person that Dad met that didn't think he was one of the greatest people in the world after they got to know him. Dad loved being a Mason and a Shriner and devoted much of his spare time to strengthening these fraternities.

To my mother Martha

Mom was my greatest cheerleader. She believed if you set your mind to something, you could accomplish the impossible. Mom was a pioneer in fighting the stereotype of women, becoming one of the top two salespeople in Saskatoon real estate. She had the ability to make people feel comfortable and help them take that next big step in life, no matter what it was.

Introduction

"SO WHAT'S IT LIKE TO BE THE MAYOR?"

If you aspire to be a carpenter, a doctor, or a farmer, it's not difficult to find information on the role, both online and elsewhere. It's much more difficult to find out what it would be like to be a city councillor or mayor. As a result, many people run for public office without remotely understanding what they're getting into. In 1994, I was one of those people.

The first reason I wrote this book was to give those who are considering running for

> The mayor's role is not an entry level position.

office a clear understanding of what they are "getting into."

1

The second reason I wrote this book was to give readers an understanding of the life of a politician, to learn a little bit about what it's like to be someone who is willing to suffer the slings and arrows of outrageous critics to make their community, province, and country a better place.

The third reason for "Building Bridges" was to explore the history of the development of the city I chose to serve – Saskatoon. History is important, and so much of it can easily be lost; we may know what happened, but we don't always know the why or the how – the stuff that helps us connect the dots and assists us in making good decisions in the future. Imagine if John Lake had written a memoir about coming to the banks of the South Saskatchewan River to establish his colony. Imagine if we could read about the thoughts of Sid Buckwold regarding his work to replace the rail yards in downtown Saskatoon?

I hope my recollections will be of value in providing the perspective of one who was directly and passionately involved with one of the most transformative periods in Saskatoon's progression.

> If you do not know the past, how can you move forward into the future?

I never thought of myself as being someone special – the mayor – but rather as an ordinary citizen who was tapped on the shoulder and given the opportunity and responsibility to uphold the standards and duties of the Office of the Mayor. I am pleased that I had the opportunity to play a role in many of the accomplishments of Saskatoon

City Council during my time in office. I hope my personal account – my colour commentary on what happened on the field – will augment the ongoing story of how our City of Saskatoon has evolved into the great Canadian city — the great global city — that I love and have proudly served.

(Anyone hoping this memoir will be a tell-all account will be disappointed. I have no interest in seeking revenge, revealing secrets, or creating a sensation. Quite the opposite. This project has given me the opportunity to express my admiration and gratitude to those who have contributed significantly to our city. Without their belief in Saskatoon, much of what is to be described would not have been possible.)

Sports

IT WAS AN EASY SHOT FROM THE BLUE LINE.

I should have stopped it. I didn't. Here I was, a 24-year-old prairie boy in Johnstown, Pennsylvania, 3,000 kms away from home, playing goalie for the NHL Pittsburgh Penguins' farm team, the Jets, in front of the home crowd. At 6'2", I towered over the net, but at that moment, I felt very small, and very alone.

The Johnstown Jets was the team that inspired the Hollywood movie *Slap Shot*, a 1977 film about an unruly group of players who spent more time brawling than skating. Their fans were no less outrageous, especially when their goalie failed to stop a shot that, according to them at least, anybody's kid sister could have handled. The abuse flew at me like a hailstorm, with much of it relating to my mother. (They never go after your father, have you noticed?)

Little did I realize at the time how experiences like this would help prepare me for civic politics.

Growing up in Saskatoon, I was always committed to sports, especially hockey and football. I was a big kid right from the day I was born in 1952. When I was six, my first two-wheeler broke in half shortly after I got it, and my dad had to have it repaired and reinforced. (It's something I still get teased about to this day.)

I attended Queen Elizabeth (Grades 1-4) and Holliston (Grades 5-8) public elementary schools. In those days, one of the annual sports highlights was the East-West hockey game. Organized by the public school system, the game pitted the best players from the east side of the river against the best players from the west side of the river. Something like an all-star game, it was a really big deal for the kids who were chosen to play in it. We were even given time off from school to attend practices. I was the East Side's goalie. (By the way, our team won.)

The next fall, I started at Walter Murray Collegiate and my size, well beyond that of most 14-year-olds, immediately attracted the interest of the football coaches. Although I was just in Grade Nine, I made the junior team. I still recall how anxious I was the day they posted the list of who was going to be a Walter Murray Marauder. My heart sank as I read the list from the top down, with no "Atchison" to be found. (With a name starting with "A," if my name was on the list, it usually was at the top.) Then, at the very bottom, there it was – the last name!

I loved football. My favourite position, and where I thought I did my best, was offensive left tackle — one of the most important positions in football because the player's job is to protect the blind side of his quarterback. In Grade Eleven, I was named Rookie of the Year on the senior team. In my last year, I was co-captain and played the entire game as an offensive and defensive lineman, and on special teams. One special team involved both the kicking team (the kicking off of the ball at the start of the game) and the receiving team (which naturally tries to take the ball all the way back for a touchdown, even though that goal seldom happens). Then there is the punting team — put into play when the team hasn't made a first down and the ball is too far out of range to kick a field goal. The ball is punted away so it is further away from your goal line. I was on the punt return team; when the ball was kicked to us, we would try to get as close as possible to the opposition's goal line. Finally, there is the field goal team — when the team doesn't get a first down but is in range to put the ball through the uprights on the field for three points.

I played the entirety of every game. I asked the coaches to give some of the other players, who were on the bench, a chance to play. These special teams all require an extended amount of running, up to 100 yards at a time, so it could be quite exhausting, But the

Compromise, understanding, and a sense of humor will get us through a lot of situations.

coaches said when someone could play better than I did, they would play them — until then, I was to continue playing the full game.

But when it comes to sports, it's not my athletic accomplishments that I cherish most. It's the life lessons I learned. When you think about it, playing the positions I did, meant that I wasn't the player actually scoring the points. As a football lineman, I rarely touched the ball — and in all the years I played hockey, I never scored a goal. However, I understood how my role was important to the team; in hockey, if I let the puck get past me, I felt I had let down the fans and the entire team. Those lessons proved essential in civic politics, where the ability is to get everyone moving in the same direction, sharing the same vision; it's about consensus, not control.

As big as I was, I never wanted to get into fights and I remember only two. In one, I was more of an unwilling assistant than a combatant. I was in Indiana with the Fort Wayne Komets. (Along with the Jets, the Komets and the Hershey Bears were farm teams for the Pittsburgh Penguins. The Hershey Bears are in Hershey, Pennsylvania, and are owned by the Hershey Chocolate Company. Hershey is one of the largest chocolate manufacturers in the world. Fort Wayne, Indiana, known to some as Fort Rainy as the weather systems would come off Lake Michigan and head southeast to Fort Wayne, was the home to International Harvester, Magnavox, a GE plant, and a railway hub. Also home to avid, blue-collar hockey fans.)

In 2018, on a visit to Fort Wayne to commemorate the Komets win of the 1972-73 Turner Cup championship, several people thanked me for providing great entertainment and winning the championship. The starting goaltender in those playoffs, Robbie Irons, broke his thumb in the first playoff game. I was called upon to play and we won all the games in the playoffs with the exception of one game in Flint, Michigan in overtime. Eleven victories — one loss.

As backup goalie on the bench for that first playoff game, my main role was cheerleader. After two periods, our team and our rivals had only one goal in mind: bloodying the noses of the opposition. That was achieved early in the third period in a full-scale brawl. Our guys streamed over the benches — despite the protests of our coach. The other team's bench had cleared and everyone started swinging – except for me. I looked down the bench and realized I was the only one not on the ice. I knew I had to get out there, but I wasn't really keen on doing so. Hockey brawls can be extremely dangerous. Rather than leap across the boards, I lumbered over to the gate. Not being in any particular hurry, I stepped warily onto the ice.

I really didn't want to square off with anyone, so I looked around to see where I could help my teammates. For the rest of the brawl, I would find an opposing player who was on top of one of our guys and haul him off in the full Nelson that I learned from wrestling. At that point, one

Some say there is not a solution to every problem, but we must try.

of our guys, seeing an opportunity, would start punching my captive while I held him. As soon as I sensed the poor sucker was ready to call it a day, I would let him go and repeat the procedure with another opposing player. Much to my surprise, my teammates later talked about what a hero I was, even though I never threw one punch the entire fight. As I used to tell my friends, "I'm a lover, not a fighter!"

I was never a hot-head, either. The one time I lost my cool, I learned another lesson. It was a Sunday night game in Brandon, Manitoba with the Western Hockey League. I was outraged that the referee allowed a questionable goal scored on me. I kept yelling at the ref as I followed him all the way to the blue line. That fit of anger drained me physically and emotionally and for the remainder of the game, I couldn't focus. I know now why some cultures regard rage as a sign of weakness; it is an emotion that takes

> Great coaches help you understand what you do in relation to everyone else and make sure everyone keeps their eyes on the prize.

away your ability to optimally perform. So even in the most heated debates in City Council, I tried to keep cool.

Goalies who want to be in the NHL have to learn much more than how to stop a puck. It is essential for a goaltender to analyze players, not only on opposing teams, but also on their own team. These analytical skills are useful for goalies long after their playing days on the ice have come to an end. Many goaltenders who have had experiences similar to mine have gone on to be coaches or leaders in business and public life — former Montreal Canadiens' Ken Dryden, who became a federal cabinet minister, comes to mind.

Just as in sports, when I became mayor, I did not get to pick my team, but I had to analyze and work with my team. Reading other people was very valuable to me as a member of Saskatoon City Council and as mayor. Before a vote was held on a particular issue, I was confident I knew how each councillor would vote. I would sometimes write down my prediction and was disappointed in myself afterwards if I misjudged a councillor's decision. I asked myself, "What did I miss? How can I learn more about this person?"

Playing team sports like football made me realize the importance of getting everyone to play together – not just playing their positions, but playing their positions to complement and inspire others on the team. That unity is not easy to achieve, as you can see so often in both sports and politics.

My coaches encouraged me to take a run at becoming a professional football player after high school. But as important as sports had become in my life, my education was also important, both to me as well as my parents. I went straight from Grade Twelve to enrolling in the University of Saskatchewan.

I tried out that fall for a position with the major junior hockey team, the Saskatoon Blades. I structured my schedule so I could both play hockey and fit my required classes in. In the end, I didn't make the Blades and was about to accept the position of back-up goalie for the University of Saskatchewan's Huskies when Malcolm Stelk, the coach of the Junior B Saskatoon Macs (which became the Quakers) asked me to be the starting goaltender for his team. We had a very successful season, culminating in playing in the 1971 Canada Winter Games. The next year, I was invited back to the Blades' training camp and was finally chosen as their starting goalie.

As my university studies intensified, I needed to choose between football and hockey. I would have liked to have played with the U of S's Huskie football team, but I needed to be realistic about my chances of playing a pro sport. My chances in professional hockey were far better, and frankly more lucrative, than pro football. My future on the ice looked promising.

I was working in our family's clothing store in 1972 when a call came from sportscaster Ed Kelly at CFQC-TV, telling me that I had just been drafted by the Pittsburgh Penguins. I had been doing well at university, especially in my marketing classes, but the news in that phone call meant that my current academic education was over.

After being drafted by the Pittsburgh Penguins, I was sent down to play on their farm teams. As well as Johnstown, Pennsylvania, I played for the Komets Fort Wayne, Indiana and then with the Hershey Bears in Hershey, Pennsylvania. The closest I came to reaching my

NHL dream was when I was scheduled to play a game in Pittsburgh, only to be told an hour before game warm-up that Gary Innis would be in goal instead. It was clear that the Penguins had ranked me as their number three goaltender, and I knew what was in the cards.

I loved playing. I couldn't believe I was actually getting paid to play the sport I loved. I saw many other players who didn't enjoy the game at all — it was work. They had lost their love for the game, yet they couldn't or wouldn't leave it. For some it was about choice. If they didn't play hockey, what would they do? Become sanitary engineers, or get a job driving a Coca-Cola™ or beer delivery? Others had no idea what they would do with the rest of their life — the only plan they had was hockey, the only dream, the NHL. The pressure on them to perform was tremendous. Some players were married and had children — families that were counting on Dad to do well. These players had nothing to fall back on. But I did.

At age 24, I could either spend several more years on farm teams, hoping to get my break, or I could hang up my skates and head home. I could have a job back in the family business tomorrow if I wanted to and my dad was certainly hoping I would come back and ask for one. I headed back to Saskatoon to work at our store in the Grosvenor Park Shopping Centre, but not without lingering thoughts of those players who were not so lucky with choices — especially for those with the pressure of a family and not knowing how they would provide for them if they didn't perform well. In sports, it's Darwin's Theory — survival of the fittest. There is always someone coming up in the ranks who wants your position. It's all about winning and if you don't win, changes have to be made. It is a cruel reality, but in sports it's all about winning.

I still loved hockey. I became coach and later owner of the North Saskatchewan Junior B League's Saskatoon Quakers. We went to the Canada Winter Games in Brandon, Manitoba. We did okay, but we didn't medal. To a great degree, medaling is what the Games are all about, but teaching the players values and instilling confidence in them was equally important. The event brought back memories of when I represented Saskatchewan in the Canada Winter Games in Saskatoon as a goalie and the positive media attention that accompanied it.

After the Winter Games in Brandon, I decided I needed a stronger team so we could return in four years to the Games. To do that, I took the team to Europe and played exhibition games in different countries in order to recruit the players with the level of talent I needed. We played in Germany and Austria on the first trip. It was a success for recruiting and developing friendships, and, of course, the Europeans naturally wanted to see North American hockey teams play. The second year, we took the team to Sweden, Finland, and Russia and began to make plans for exhibition games in Japan for the following year.

But once more — a telephone call changed my plans.

Blades' General Manager Daryl Lubiniecki (Lubie) asked if I would consider being their goaltending coach. This was a first; no team had ever had a coach only for two players — the goaltenders. We had tremendous success — and that success went beyond the Blades. Almost all the goaltenders went on to successful careers in sports, whether as a player in the NHL, or as a sports broadcaster, or even as a golf professional. It was extremely fulfilling to see each and every one of them trying to accomplish their dream of being in the NHL.

When Lorne Molleken, a former goalie, became the Blades' head coach, I became, as they say, redundant. When Lubie called me to tell me that Lorne was going to coach the goaltenders as well as the rest of the team, I said I was fine with that decision. Lubie became quite upset and asked me, "Don't you realize how close you are to being in the NHL as a coach — just one step away?"

I responded that I didn't have that realization, but I wished the team well. We discussed how we could work it out for me to return to the coach role, but I said, "You have made the decision. I understand. And I don't want there to be any second thoughts later on."

By then, I had had enough hockey. My NHL dreams had long since faded and I settled into the good life of my home town and focused on our retail store.

(The year I went to work with the Blades, I received a phone call from Greg Dionne, asking if I would sell the Quakers to him. I didn't sell Greg the team — I gave him the team. Ironically, Greg would later become a city councillor in Prince Albert and eventually become the mayor of his city. How about that — two city mayors coming from the Quakers!)

Suits

THOSE WHO THINK THAT RUNNING A small business is easy money have never owned, or been part of a family that owned, a small business. When my father first left the army, he worked at Mac and Mac's menswear in Regina. Seeing this was not lucrative enough to raise a family, he hired on with the CNR as a fireman and later became an engineer. But he loved the men's clothing industry, and so when a slowdown in rail occurred and shifts became sparse, he moved his family to Saskatoon where he worked for several menswear stores and learned the industry. In 1971, he and my mother bought a men's clothing store and named it *Mr. Atch & Sons*.

My parents were very social and service-oriented, which is why they were successful as small business owners.

They worked hard and their work ethic rubbed off on me. My dad would be off to work, including Saturdays, looking after customers, looking after inventory, looking after lease payments, looking after staffing, looking after cleaning and maintenance – looking after everything, it seemed, often well into the night. My mother started working when I was in Grade Six, first in cosmetics at the

> What everyone is looking for in their lives, regardless of where they live, is hope, joy, trust and faith.

Co-Op, then in real estate — a career which she left to work full-time in the store.

Growing up, I learned about the importance of not just getting customers — but also keeping them. My dad would often say, "If you don't look after the customer, someone else will." In the men's clothing business, customer loyalty is the key to success; we knew there were only so many people in our community who would pay for the quality of products we were offering.

Perhaps because owning a store sounds glamorous, or perhaps because my dad and his employees, including me, wore expensive business suits — whatever the reason, all too often we, and other small business owners, would be stereotyped as being big business, elite, and not in tune with the average working person. Nothing could be further from the truth, as the neighbours of our small house on 2nd Street could attest.

The fact is, there were many months when money was tight. During those more profitable months, we were too busy to enjoy the extra cash. We were not part of Saskatoon's "rich and famous," although we certainly had some very influential and highly regarded corporate leaders as customers. For friendship and socializing, my parents enjoyed their connection with the Shriners, and on Sundays, the members of the congregation at the small Lutheran church we attended on 8th Street and Dufferin Avenue.

I liked going to church. I still do. I'm proud to be a Christian, just as others should be proud of their faith in our multicultural country. My parents told me they would not have been surprised if I had gone into the ministry, like my uncle. He had gone to Denver to study dentistry but ended up joining the Lutheran seminary. (I remember being quite excited to receive a birthday

> Some like to box groups up and label them, I like to look at everyone as their own person.

present in the mail from him when I turned ten, only to be less than thrilled when I saw it was a Bible.) I can owe my brief acting career to the church as well. One year, in the St. Paul's Lutheran Church Christmas play, I was a skirt-wearing Roman soldier!

I was taught to be respectful of other people's beliefs. Yes, I participated in the Mayor's Prayer Breakfast, but I also participated in many celebrations and events of other religions.

If I seem somewhat strict in my conduct, it's because I like to live by basic rules, especially those

I learned growing up. In the 1960s, I was the good kid next door that your parents might have pointed to when complaining about your rebellious conduct. (Sorry about that.) I really wasn't trying to be the poster child for short hair and unquestioned obedience to one's elders — it just happened that way.

I think my personality was shaped by the fact that my parents had lost two children before I was born, and perhaps were over-protective of me. The other factor, I'm sure, is that being such a big lad, I was always expected to be careful not to hurt the other kids I played with.

When I started high school in 1966, boys were getting suspended for having their hair too long, and girls were being sent home because their dresses were too short. Hit songs like *Wild Thing, Yellow Submarine,* and *19th Nervous Breakdown* were being pumped out by the Beatles, the Rolling Stones, and countless other bands with psychedelic names. The whole free love, hippy movement was getting rolling, culminating in Woodstock the year I began Grade Twelve. As for me, I had already adopted the values and attitudes I had been taught by my coaches, teachers, and parents. I was never rebellious. I never drank or smoked (cigarettes or anything else!). I never even had a favourite rock band, preferring instead the easy listening sounds of Ray Conniff, The New Seekers, and Sergio Mendes & Brasil '66.

Rather than being one of the guys who got kicked out of school for wearing their hair too long, I successfully ran for Student Representative Council and was on the Honour Roll. My favourite subjects were maths and sciences, but I was keen to take as many classes as I could. While my classmates were skipping classes to hang out at the Coachman Restaurant in nearby Market Mall, I was taking electives like accounting over the noon hour, without any urging from my parents.

As further proof of how uncool I was, I had a summer job as a Fuller Brush salesman when I was 19, going door to door, never sure what I would encounter. Talk about ideal training for door-knocking as a mayoralty candidate! My days on the ice had thickened my skin, which is what you definitely need as a door-knocking salesman or a politician. I remember training a rookie salesman who was shadowing me on one of my routes. The guy was surprised at how I could shake off whatever abuse would come our way, and how I would simply turn to him and say, "Well, on to the next. We just got one door closer to a sale!" This taught me that if you're not afraid of rejection, if you can keep knocking on doors, you can find success.

Just as my family was what you could call average mainstream church-goers, it's also fair to say they were not very political, and certainly not openly political. When you're in the retail business, it's best to keep your thoughts on controversial subjects to yourself. We were just as happy to suit up a Liberal father of the

Issues don't go away just because you ignore them.

bride as we were a Conservative best man or an NDP groom. We never attended any political rallies, never had lawn signs. For many years, I got more emotional over the Stanley Cup than any election — civic or otherwise.

However, my sense of community commitment is a completely different matter – and one that some have difficulty distinguishing from politics. I remember becoming quite interested in the idea of democratic elections while in Grade Six, thanks to my teacher Miss Schmidt. We followed the British election that year, and I learned to appreciate the power of the ballot. More than anything, though, my sense of civic duty came from my parents' involvement in our community, our sports teams, our school, and in the goings-on of civic government as it related to our business.

> We need to have big ideas and bold actions that benefit the city as a whole.

Hardened political activists might scoff at the idea, but I see no reason why you have to belong to a political party in order to make a positive difference in your community and to bring about change that is good for everyone, regardless of their political, cultural, or religious affiliations. Who doesn't benefit, for example, from clean drinking water?

A man who is being fitted for a suit is often accompanied by a wife, partner, or friend and the length of the activity provides ample time to talk. Working in the store, I listened to all points of view about all kinds of

ATCHISON

issues from all sorts of people and soon realized there can be more than one reasonable side to an issue.

Working in the store also gave me the time to think about civic issues in particular, and to me they seemed more real, more immediate, than federal or provincial matters. Changes to our constitution are important, certainly, but they don't bang your wheels out of alignment like driving through a pothole. If we need a bridge, why not build one? Libraries are real. Swimming pools are real. Housing is real. Municipal politics has the greatest effect upon the quality of life for the residents.

Sometimes my solutions would strike others as downright ludicrous, such as my suggestion that we build a dome over 21st Street to create a year-round climate-controlled shopping area. But why not think big in Saskatoon, when in fact, these domes are being built in other places? You can bet that West Edmonton Mall had its own contingent of detractors when it was first suggested — but through constructive partnerships, it was built.

Just because civic issues can often be about the immediate – the here and now – does not mean citizens and politicians should be limited in their vision. Short-sightedness can hurt cities in the long run and unfortunately those who think too politically are concerned only about what happens during their four-year term. I have seen too many politicians who became obsessed with re-election and

We can't change the past, but we can create the future together.

didn't think beyond it — focusing on the glory of next term instead of achieving in the present one.

During my thirteen years as mayor, I was never a member of any political party, even though I was asked at different times by all three major political parties to run in their federal or provincial campaigns — or to endorse particular candidates. In all cases, I declined. I give full kudos, though, to those civic councillors like Randy Donauer and Eric Olauson who were willing to risk their position on Council to run during federal and provincial elections.

I just don't think of myself as political in the traditional sense. Up until 1994, running for any elected position was the farthest thing from my mind.

At the beginning of that year, I was 42, working full-time in the store, and very happy to be Mardele's husband and the father of five great kids. We had close friends and great neighbours. We were content with paying a mortgage, participating in community activities, and quietly living our lives according to our values. In short, life was good. The only time I really paid attention to politics, civic or otherwise, was if it had a direct impact on my business or family — pretty much like most people.

Back in the '70s, City Council meetings were not broadcasted on television. Most times, you waited for the latest news report from CFQC-TV reporter Terry Higgins who was positioned outside of Council chambers. In other words, most people had no idea what a council meeting was really like. As for me, I was inside those chambers only once prior to being on Council. I had gone, at the urging of my father and other downtown retailers, to speak on the issue of store hours. Certainly, though, I had no thoughts about running for Council, much less becoming mayor.

My, how things can change.

Nominations Close
On Wednesday

ON MONDAY, SEPTEMBER 26TH, 1994, MY wife, Mardele and I sat down in our family room to watch CTV's local 6 p.m. news. Newscaster Rob MacDonald announced the Saskatoon civic election had been called for Wednesday, October 26th.

It had been a very tough year for the city, and the situation had come to a head in mid-August when, after two years of unsuccessful bargaining, the four Canadian Union of Public Employees (CUPE) locals — along with transit workers (ATU), electrical workers (IBEW), and the police association — began various actions, leading to the largest-public sector strike in Saskatchewan's history. The police went on strike, CUPE members walked out in sympathy, and the City locked out workers. The police reached a settlement and returned to work, but it would be ten weeks before the remaining 2,300 workers agreed to a new contract. The solidarity shown by members of the unions was almost unparalleled; during the long disagreement, not one person crossed a picket line, even though many faced severe financial stress. There was a high degree of public support for the strikers, as well, with donations over $100,000 flowing in from across the country.

Dignity is economic freedom.

I shared the widespread opinion that our City and its council were in disarray. I also thought the lengthy strike and the pain it caused was the fault of both sides.

Fortunately for the incumbent mayor, Henry Dayday, the disputes were settled before the upcoming election. He was seeking a third term and he and all the Council incumbents were in a tough race. Dayday was being challenged by seven other candidates, including high-profile, well-organized mayoralty hopefuls like Councillor Mark Thompson, businessman Bob Lacoursiere, and community activist Sandra Mitchell. In total, there were 110 candidates running in the election for the different positions of mayor, councillor, and school board trustee.

One reason for the high number of candidates was the recent change by the provincial NDP government, re-introducing civic elections by ward. In the previous eleven civic elections, all of the incumbents running for mayor and councillor were elected. One of the reasons, it was argued, was that every candidate was running against every other candidate city-wide, making it difficult for a newcomer to break through. After all, who would have the time or the money to campaign across the entire city? With the ward system legislated in the spring of 1994, a candidate would know that he or she would be running against only one incumbent, and could concentrate on campaigning just in their ward.

One of the issues in 1994 was the proposed transfer of downtown, city-owned land to provide a site for a casino and trade and convention facility. (I hasten to add this wasn't the huge controversy over the SIGA [Saskatchewan Indian Gaming Authority] casino that arose in 2002/2003.) A petition opposing the transfer (and thus preventing the casino from being built downtown) had been circulated successfully, resulting in a referendum for the civic election. I, like many others, was opposed to a downtown casino.

Understandably, there were strident opinions being voiced in the community about the casino, the strikes, and other issues. As a retailer, I heard arguments on all sides from our customers. Like many of my fellow retailers and neighbours, I became increasingly concerned about how the city was being managed. I felt the handling of the strike, especially, was a sign of a council in disarray.

There were those, myself included, who felt that part of the problem was the absence of business-minded

> You need leaders to stand up when things are difficult.

people on Council. "We need the voice of business at City Hall," my friends would say. But, of course, no one was willing to let their name stand.

Mardele had also heard me repeat these sentiments more than a few times and when the TV newscaster announced that nominations for the civic election would close in two days, she turned to me and said, "I think you should run. You would do a good job."

> Destiny is not a matter of chance – it is a matter of choice.

Somewhat to my own surprise, that's all the encouragement I needed. The next day, I picked up the nomination form, which required a small deposit and 25 signatures from eligible voters in my ward. The deposit was no problem, but I remember how uncomfortable I was asking for those signatures. Not only was I not used to being openly political, I only had 24 hours to get the signatures. Even so, by Wednesday at 4 p.m., I was officially a candidate to represent Ward 10 in the 1994 Civic Election.

In those days, there was no "Civic Elections for Dummies" guide. I remember City Clerk Janice Mann simply handing the nomination papers to me — and that was it. Likewise, there was no manual to tell you what you would be signing up for — all the committees you would be expected to be on, the hours of meetings, the phone calls to be made and answered, and the amount of reading that would be involved. You had to learn as you went along.

There were six other candidates running for Ward

10, which included the neighbourhoods of Sutherland, Forest Grove, Erindale, College Park, and the newly-developed Silver Spring. Leading the pack of candidates was Peter Prebble, a very adept politician who was first elected as an NDP candidate in the 1978 provincial election, was defeated in the next provincial election, then won again in 1986. His civic election bio stated he was an environmental researcher who had served as an MLA for eight years. He was well-known, well-organized, a confident speaker, and well-versed in campaigning. I, on the other hand, was the opposite.

In city politics, people vote for individuals, not political parties.

For the most part, my first campaign was a one-man show. I had absolutely zero experience with election campaigns, at any level. I had no war chest of money for posters, billboards, or other campaign materials. Although I certainly appreciated the help of Barb and Willie Grieve, who lived a few doors away and were very experienced with political campaigns, I had no official campaign organizers. What I did have, though, was a determination to do everything I could to get elected.

My first day of door-knocking was an eye-opener. Over the years, our business had spent tens of thousands of dollars on advertising. Everybody would know the name Atchison, right? Wrong! How dismayed I was to discover almost every homeowner I talked to didn't know who I was and didn't care. I felt like all that money my father and I had spent on advertising Mr. Atch & Sons was a complete waste!

In civic politics, especially, name recognition is important. As a candidate for mayor or city council, you are on your own. You cannot rely on the popularity of your party or political leader to get you elected, and you have no provincial or national machine to run big ad campaigns. So how was I, an unknown candidate, going to get noticed in the four weeks I had before the election — especially when I was running against a front-runner that everyone knew, in a ward where there were six other candidates to split the vote? My answer: Burma Shave.

In Saskatoon, we are not only dreamers, but we are also doers.

In the 1950s, Burma Shave (a men's shaving cream) came up with the idea of advertising their product through catchy signs posted along the highways of America. Basically, it's how billboard advertising works: you pinpoint high-traffic routes and capitalize on the number of people who drive by and notice your signs. If it worked for Burma Shave, it could work for me. With my campaign placard in hand, I stepped out the door at 5 a.m. and headed for the corner of McKercher and Boychuk to catch the morning commuter traffic.

It's something that most people would be very uncomfortable doing, but I didn't hesitate. If you can stand in the goal crease in a packed arena, you can certainly stand on a street-corner with a sign in one hand, and wave at passersby with the other. It worked. Some people would even honk to show support.

As election day drew closer, the days of autumn became shorter and colder, but I kept at my sign-holding, arm-waving, street-corner strategy for both the morning and the afternoon drive times. On some of those mornings, standing out there in my business suit left me chilled to the bone. My solution was to wear a sandwich board, because then I could wear a parka over my suit and under the two slats of cardboard. I added Central Avenue and Attridge Drive to my strategic locales, then Central Avenue and College Drive.

I tried to make eye contact with as many people as I could. That was just as important as my sandwich board. It's surprising how effectively eye contact can confirm in others that you are sincere, that you care.

Oscar Wilde once said, "It's better to be talked about than not talked about." Songwriter and producer of more than fifty Broadway musicals, George M. Cohan's message to a newspaper reporter was, "I don't care what you say about me, as long as you say something about me, and as long as you spell my name right." So, all those people driving into work every morning — to office buildings, construction sites, warehouses, machine shops — some of them started the morning coffee conversation with, "Did you see that big guy wearing the sandwich board, waving on the street corner?"

I think people received the message that, even

though my tactic might be corny, my commitment was sincere. I was hoping they would see someone who was willing to stick his neck out, to stand up and be counted, even if it meant standing out in the cold in the early morning, every workday, without fail. Those wonderful people who stopped to bring me coffee — whether out of a feeling of support or sympathy — warmed my heart as well as my hands!

There were other times, though, when I was not standing alone. It made my day when someone would call me to say I had made the right decision to run. I remember a phone call with Murray McMaster, who was battling cancer at the time. "What are you going to run on?" he asked, so I outlined my platform. The next day, he showed up at the store with a complete layout for a poster and brochure.

I put that material to good use. (I'm partly to blame for how advertising has increased in Saskatoon's civic elections.) In addition to my Burma Shave drive time campaigning, I spent my evenings going door to door, handing out my brochures.

> It's businesses that drive the economy.

Although I talked to hundreds of people, my only promise was to work as hard as I could in the best interests of my ward and city. I was straightforward. Sometimes, people would ask me to promise something we both knew was completely unrealistic. Perhaps they were testing me. I answered truthfully. I'm not the silver-

tongued orator who can verbally dance around a subject
— but then again, I never wanted to be.

One issue, for my ward in particular, was a proposed
grade separation, such as an underpass or overpass, for the
railway crossing on Central Avenue in the neighbourhood
of Sutherland. Anyone
who lives in that part
of Saskatoon knows the
frustration of waiting for
the slow-moving train to cross Central. From what I recall,
most (if not all) of the candidates said they were in favour
of a grade separation. I think their main motivation was
to not be singled out. Many political candidates are like
that, I have found. I, however, said I was not in favour of
the rail separation, that it was too expensive for what it
would accomplish. To me, the best answer was to get the
railway to move the line. My refusal to commit to a grade
separation wasn't popular, but people told me later they
at least knew I was being straight with them, and not just
saying something to get elected.

Politicians think of
the next election,
statesmen think of the
next generation.

I was different from Peter Prebble and the other
candidates in other ways. I was proud to be a businessman.
I was up front about being a Mason and a Director of the
Riverside Country Club. I wore a business suit for my
campaign picture, when I campaigned door-to-door, and
when appearing in any of the candidate debates. To me, it
was a simple decision for voters. Take me or leave me; the
choice is yours. But if you do elect me, you'll know who I

am.

In hindsight, the fact I was largely unknown was also an advantage. Peter Prebble had considerable political baggage, and there was no way he could distance himself from the New Democratic Party (not that he wanted to) in a civic election. Compared to the other candidates, I was a clear choice. As election day drew closer, I was emerging as Peter's main contender.

Drawing attention to yourself isn't always a positive. People can get pretty emotional. I would go to one doorstep and be told by the homeowner they would never vote for me because I was a business person. On the next doorstep, I would be told we needed more business people like me on City Council. People would let me know what they thought, not only at candidate meetings and

A healthy and strong democracy is just not possible if we live in fear of expressing our views.

on the doorstep, but also when they came into the store. My venture into politics lost us customers, including ones that had been very loyal prior to my terms as councillor and mayor.

I not only lost customers, I lost friends – or should I say, people I thought were friends. I found out who my real friends were, not so much based on whether or not they voted for me; your vote, after all, is a very private matter. It was more a question of whether or not they would at least encourage me, thank me for running, or say to Mardele and others that I was doing the right thing.

My decision to run was a surprise for my parents. My father thought I was crazy to run for office. I remember walking into the store after filing my nomination papers. My dad was on the main floor. When I told him what I had done, he shouted, "Why would you want to go and do that for?", adding one of his favourite expletives. He understood, better than I, what it would mean to the store not only in terms of public reaction to my candidacy, but also what it would mean if I won. He told me, "Politics and business don't mix." I disagreed. To me, the skills you learn in business, and the perspective you gain from listening to your customers, are very much in tune with running a city. (Despite his misgivings about my choice, however, he stood by me, just as he has always done.)

Then, I went down to the store's lower level to tell my mother. "You should have run 20 years ago," she said, adding that she was "tickled pink" with my decision. Thank goodness for moms!

For Mardele and our five children, my entry into civic politics exposed them to things I hadn't anticipated when I acted upon my impulse to become a candidate. The kids were between seven and seventeen at the time, and for the next 22 years – during my terms as councillor and mayor – they would sometimes have to hear less than kind remarks about their father in the media, on the schoolground, and on the street.

A thick skin is not something you can pass on to your offspring. Personally, I could take the mean-spirited comments. I saw it as part of the job, just like being a professional hockey player. But you can never get used to the effect those comments have on your wife and kids. I wonder if people today who use social media to viciously and blindly attack a public person ever stop to think about the effect of their attack.

As Wednesday, October 26th drew nearer, I began to feel more confident about my chances. I remember one of my opposing candidates coming up to me just days before the election. "You're going to win," he said. "Even my own father says he's voting for you!"

I was such a novice that I never even thought to host a get-together on election night. Mardele and I stayed home to watch the election coverage on television. Then my friend Willie Grieves called me, saying that because I had won Sutherland, I would win the ward. I was still unconvinced; I had been involved in more than one game where it looked like it was in the bag, only to end in an upset. Then, the media started calling, and the television commentators declared me the winner in Ward 10, with a margin of almost 600 votes over Peter Prebble. I realized I better get down to City Hall.

By the end of the night, it was clear that Saskatoon's citizens wanted change in how their city was run. The turnout (45% of the 144,000 eligible voters) was the highest in the city's history. The casino issue about the transfer of property was rejected with 50,938 voting "no" versus just 13,182 in favour. Henry Dayday came close to losing his bid for a third term as mayor; it wasn't until almost three hours after polls closed that he was declared winner over Sandra Mitchell. Three of the incumbents – including Glen Penner, who had been on Council for 13 years, and Bev Dyck, who had been there for nine — lost their seats, and Mark Thompson was also gone, having failed in his bid for mayor. In total, there were seven new faces elected to City Council, including mine.

Among the candidates at City Hall that night was Peter Prebble. He congratulated me, saying, "You worked harder." I very much appreciated that comment, which demonstrated once again the quality of Peter's character. Although we have disagreed on various issues, I have always respected him and call him a friend.

I remember a time after the election, when Peter had been re-elected to the provincial government. He invited me to his constituency Christmas party. When I walked in the room, there

> We don't do what's easy, we do what's right.

were people there — friends of Peter's and hard-core NDP supporters — who were surprised, if not dismayed, to see me. I guess Peter must have heard some comments, because during his remarks to everyone he said, "I want you to know I invited Councillor Don Atchison. I'm glad he could join us today." That is my definition of a class act.

The morning after the election, I was back on the street corners, waving thank you during the morning and evening drives. Back at home, Mardele had a question for me. "I was wondering," she said. "How much do you get paid for being on Council?"

I had no idea. I had never thought to ask.

Learning The Ropes

THE DAY AFTER THE 1994 SASKATOON civic election, I awoke at my usual time of 6 a.m., eager to start my new job as a member of Saskatoon City Council. The problem was, I had no idea of what I was supposed to do. We were told by the City Clerk to show up the Monday following the election at 7 p.m. sharp. When I arrived, I saw that the seating had been arranged according to ward numbers. As the new councillor for Ward 10, I was the last to be sworn in.

The voters of Saskatoon had wanted new faces on council, and their wish was certainly granted. Seven of the ten councillors were rookies. In addition to myself, there was Myles Heidt, Herve Langlois, Rick Steernberg, Anita Langford, Jill Postlethwaite, and Patricia Roe. Although we

ATCHISON

were told there would be an orientation session for the new councillors, we were given no handbook or other reference material on procedures or policies. In fairness to the staff, there had never been such a turnover in the past. (I thought it strange that Mayor Dayday didn't attend the orientation — not even for the few minutes it would have taken to make us feel welcome and encourage us. Although I came to appreciate the advice he offered later on, especially his thoughts on the role of mayor.)

The orientation session was no pep rally! The information was delivered unenthusiastically and with little encouragement. I received the clear message that city administration expected the new councillors to tow the line and to not rock the boat. As if to keep us in our place, one of the City Hall staffers told us newcomers, "Long after you're gone, your City of Saskatoon staff will still be here." He was wrong. Twenty years later, I would be the only one in that room who would still be around. I ran for City Council because I wanted to rock the boat — regardless of how unsettling that might be to some. I could sense the gigantic pent-up energy in our city ready to awaken.

> A healthy and strong democracy is just not possible if we live in fear of expressing our views.

That first meeting was the only time at City Hall where all I did was sit back and listen. After that, it was time to get to work.

Citizens and the media are quick to describe city

40

councillors along the two lines of "pro-business" and "pro-labour." I was categorized as the pro-business councillor, although I regarded Peter McCann and Donna Birkmaier as being pro-business as well. City Council, however, was largely pro-labour, which wasn't surprising given the labour unrest prior to the election and the urging of union members to get out and vote for specific candidates.

There were times when the vote would be 10-1, with me being the lone dissenter. One such matter was the move, led by Mayor Dayday, to change the title and responsibilities of then City Commissioner Marty Irwin to City Manager, which would give him more autonomy to make decisions on his own. I didn't like the decision; I believe the people who are

> I believe we must make tough decisions, and I have in the past; I haven't kicked the problem down the road.

elected are the ones who should be held accountable and to make the decisions. A city commissioner and mayor shared the authority. I believed to change the authority structure so a city manager could unilaterally make decisions without the input of the mayor was an abdication of responsibility by an elected leader; something a mayor might do if he or she did not want to be held accountable if things didn't go quite right during their watch – a political way of avoiding the heat. If I were the mayor, I thought, I would want the authority to get things done my way, and the responsibility that comes with that. Obviously, I was the only one on council with that point of view.

I was very curious as to how things actually worked at City Hall. We were being criticized for being top heavy in management. This criticism might have been valid — the City of Saskatoon is a corporation with some 3,000 employees, making it the second largest organization in Saskatoon, next to the Health Region — but I wasn't in a hurry to make a major change to the management structure. I was less than satisfied with what might be the motive behind the suggestion; I wanted to wait and see for myself how things ran before introducing anything radically different. I thought the rest of the new councillors should do the same, but instead they decided to move forward on the suggestion.

> You'll never know what a leader is like until they have power.

Early on, I accepted the fact that I might be the lone voice with a different point of view on an issue before City Council. That was okay by me. I wasn't about to play fast and loose with my vote just to go along with everyone else. I also wasn't interested in "making deals," as if my vote were some kind of currency. I considered my vote to be sacred. I never wanted to play the game of, "If I vote for your motion on this matter, then you have to support my motion next week."

As a new city councillor, what surprised me the most, and what still leaves me scratching my head, is how some councillors would say one thing in a private meeting, and then take a completely opposite stand at

Monday council meetings. (By then, council meetings were also televised on the local community channel Cable 10. Introducing those live telecasts was one of the best things the media ever did to spark community interest in city council meetings.) There were times when I could not believe what was coming out of the mouths of some of my City Council colleagues in public, compared to what they had been saying in closed sessions only a few days before. I loved standing up in Council and goading a councillor to explain himself or herself, with both of us knowing where they truly stood on a matter.

Councillors can differ on how they see their roles. It's one thing to be typecast as being "pro-business" or "pro-labour," but quite another to see yourself as being the champion of a particular interest group. There's no question that as the owner of a small business I held views consistent with many other retail merchants, but I never saw myself as their candidate. I was someone who had been tapped on the shoulder to serve all the people of my ward, not just those who happened to share my views. I have always seen councillors and the mayor as being in the service industry, not the political arena. Nor was I ever set up by any special interest group to be their candidate, as the meagre but broad range of donations to my election campaigns showed.

Some candidates, though, were clearly committed to "towing the party line." Some went so far as to campaign on behalf of a provincial or federal election candidate (which I never did publicly or privately) and which I feel is totally inappropriate.

There always needs to be an important distinction between how a City Council operates compared to a provincial or federal government, and that difference is transparency. In the legislature or parliament, the fierce debating and decisions of a governing party are largely made behind closed doors. Once the party decides among itself which way to go, so goes the vote. Citizens rarely get a glimpse of the in-fighting over any particular policy. Those who have served as a Member of Parliament or a Member of the Legislative Assembly will tell you that not towing the party line is a serious political offense which can jeopardize your career.

I believe that in a city council, though, citizens need each councillor to stand up and state their views, defend those views, and also — so important — be open-minded enough to change their views in this forum. That's why I proposed a concept similar to Hansard, where each councillor's statements would be recorded, so you could look back and see who said what and when on any issue. (The Hansard is the official verbatim recordings of the debates that take place in parliamentary proceedings at the federal, provincial, or territorial level of Canadian government.)

As it was, the City Clerk would record the minutes stating a decision, but not how council arrived at that decision. Although by this time, committee and council meetings were being digitally recorded, that is not the same as a written record, which permits much easier research on particular issues. No one is going to sift through hours and hours of video to find out who said what.

I suggested the Hansard idea not just to hold councillors more accountable, but also so future city councils could review issues previously debated and understand why decisions were made. Without that background, councillors may rely too heavily on just the experience and knowledge of city administration to inform their decisions, leading to the debate being steered in a particular direction.

Even though there obviously will be communication between councillors before a vote, nothing should be pre-ordained. A councillor is not a member of a political party, and should have only one loyalty: to the citizens in his or her ward specifically and to

> We want those who have had hardships to be able to go from violence to resilience, from poverty to possibility and from homelessness to hope. That is what Saskatoon should be about ... giving hope and opportunity to all.

the citizens of Saskatoon in general. They should always vote according to what they think is best for Saskatoon, regardless of what their political philosophy might be. Yes, on some things such as the smoking bylaw, I sounded pro-business when I said, "We don't need a bylaw. The provincial laws are good enough. Businesses should have the choice on whether or not they allow smoking, and then consumers can decide where to spend their money."

However, there were other matters where I would raise the ire of my business colleagues because they felt I had betrayed business interests. (Once I became mayor, I was motivated to change my position on the smoking issue and put into place what was at the time one of the strongest anti-smoking laws in North America.)

I believed the law had to be equal for all. That meant, in business, the rules had to be the same for everyone, with no exception. I wanted to ban smoking, and that meant smoking on restaurant patios that sat on either public or private property. Some city councillors thought this bylaw would be unenforceable because a person could smoke on the other side of the partition on the sidewalk but not on the restaurant side. I recognized that this new law would be controversial and restaurant owners might not like it. Also, I was aware that there was a risk of restaurants going broke and employees losing their jobs. As it turned out, the restaurants suffered for a few months but eventually business was back to normal. The owners would pull me aside and thank me for putting the law into place but wouldn't say anything publicly for fear of losing customers. (I was saddened by the fact the only restaurant I'm aware of that actually went broke due to the new bylaw was owned by a personal friend of mine. I told him I was terribly sorry that he had lost his business, but he replied, "No, thank you. The smoke wasn't good for me." He went into other ventures and has become very successful. Thank goodness.)

One example of where I thought I was the one being

pro-labour was the issue of the reconfiguration of City Hall's operations, based upon a report and recommendations from Ernst & Young. I was the sole voice speaking out against the reconfiguration, which showed in the vote of 10-1 in favour of the recommendations. Later on, when the change was being implemented, one councillor said to me, "I didn't realize that City Council had voted to eliminate all these jobs!" Despite instances like these, I was destined to be typecast as the business executive, with the interests of business in mind. But when you consider this specific situation, who was acting in the interest of the big corporation? Me, or the rest of my supposedly labour-friendly City Council?

Sometimes, when the vote went 9-2, I would joke to myself, "Yeah! I've doubled council support!"

The accessibility to city councillors is an important difference at this level of governance. There's not much of a buffer between a councillor and his or her constituents. There's no premier or party leader to take the heat, or aides or a constituency office to field the phone calls. City councillors are both visible and vulnerable. My father and his staff at Atch & Co. would sometimes be startled by a long-time customer, or complete stranger, who would open the door of the store and yell, "I'll never vote for that … again, and I'll never shop in this store again!" Those situations really bothered me, because my role as a councillor wasn't affecting just me; it was affecting the family business and our wonderful staff. Boycotting the store was unfair and uncalled for. After all, my vote on council never diminished the quality of the products we sold or the service we provided!

There were also the habitual callers (every city councillor has them) who would contact you virtually every week with a complaint or a request — informing you about how their street needed cleaning or how the neighbour kids were being careless playing basketball. You do the best you can with those kinds of calls and always treat everyone with respect, even if the caller is irrational. That's just a part of public life. As one retired councillor said to me, "It got to the point that I simply had run out of patience. That's when I knew I shouldn't run again."

I'm sure that if you ask a seasoned councillor what most surprised them after being elected for the first time, it would be the amount of time they needed to devote to their duties. Most councillors in my experience take their role very seriously, and do put in the necessary time. There were those, though, who treated being on City Council like a part-time job with only so many fixed hours to devote to their duties. Rightly or wrongly, and at significant sacrifice for my family and social life, I never saw my role as councillor or as mayor as part-time, or even nine-to-five.

One of the first clues I got as to the extent of my City Council duties was the thick bundle of reading material that each city councillor received every Thursday.

In addition to being on City Council and representing a ward, a councillor must sit on various committees and commissions. Soon after the new Council is sworn in, city councillors attend a meeting to determine who should sit on what committee. At first, I volunteered for those committees that would interfere the least with my responsibilities at the store, such as the Downtown Business Improvement District (now DTNYXE) which had evening meetings when the store was closed.

Over my three terms as a councillor, though, my interest in all facets of City Hall led me to eventually sit on all committees. My favourite was Operations, because that's the committee that best represents the activities citizens see being done for their tax dollar, activities such as sidewalk repair and snow removal.

Another of my favourite committees was Audit, where you can follow the money — how it is taken in and what it is spent on. Even when I wasn't on this committee, I attended almost all of the meetings. When other committee members asked, "Why would you want to come to an audit committee when you are not even on the committee?", my response was, "I want to learn how the City actually operates and what needs to be corrected."

You can't buy wisdom.

Sitting on those committees bolstered my confidence in my ability to lead the city, to do things the way they should be done, to change the culture, which is often defined as "the way we do things around here."

I remember when I was chair of Operations and we were discussing the overpass at Taylor Street and Circle

Drive. Our people were telling us it was a ten-year project and how they were going to complete it. They had the design up on the walls and

> I'm for all the citizens –
> we must make sure those
> least able to defend
> themselves will have us
> to stand up for them.

were explaining how they were going to schedule the work piecemeal with other projects throughout the city – a little bit here, then a little bit there – so that no one in the city would feel they were being ignored in favour of some other neighbourhood. I couldn't help myself. "You know what they really think?" I blurted. "They think you can't do the job right in the first place."

That remark did not go over well at the meeting, but I wasn't about to back down. "How much does it cost to do it your way?" I continued. After some more prodding, I got the real answer. It would end up costing about 30 per cent more than concentrating on just that one overpass and getting it done. "In other words," I said, sounding like a true retailer, "If we changed things to the way I'm suggesting, it would be like paying for three overpasses and getting the fourth one free!"

We voted on it, and the committee agreed with me. Murray Totland, who was just getting started at the time, said to me, "You better be able to get this passed in Council." I told him not to worry, and to let me deal with City Council.

As for other duties of councillors — you know what they say on the television infomercials: "But wait! There's more!" Yet another duty of city councillors was to attend functions in place of the mayor. That duty is dealt with by designating each councillor deputy mayor for a month. Fairly regularly, though, the deputy mayor would also be unable (or unwilling?) to attend, so another city councillor would be designated, often at the last minute. I gained the reputation for being the next go-to councillor on the list. I liked going to those functions, certainly not because I needed time away from home, but because I felt proud to represent the City of Saskatoon and, I hoped, to enhance whatever occasion I was attending.

Eventually, everyone working at the store learned that my being on City Council wasn't like being the coach of a local hockey team. Roughly one-quarter of my business hours were eaten up by my City Council activities. I would field about 100 calls a week, and every single one would call the store. I must confess, though, there were times when my father, in frustration, would answer and say, "He's not in right now!"

Some weeks were even more intense. After one committee meeting, where I had spoken in favour of charging homeowners a new fee for garbage pickup, my comment made it to page 3 of the local newspaper. The next morning when I walked into the store, my father yelled, "Good grief! What did you say at Council last night? The phone hasn't stopped ringing all morning!" (To be honest, his expletive phrase was a little stronger than that. I'll leave it to your imagination.)

I had a stool by the phone at the store, and that day, from the moment I walked in the door until way past closing, I was on the phone with callers, mostly irate, many of them not even in my ward. I listened. Many homeowners were experiencing excess garbage, not from their own use, but from other citizens whose garbage containers were overflowing and were putting their excess in the containers belonging to their neighbours. People believe that garbage collection should be a benefit of paying property taxes; they don't like paying for garbage removal, especially when it isn't even their garbage.

After hearing what many of the callers said, I agreed with them and changed my mind. What began as a good intention did not necessarily create a positive result.

There were other times where you just had to laugh. This diminutive but very feisty lady stormed through the door one day while I was sitting by the till. She immediately started voicing her concerns in no uncertain terms while I, like a gentleman, stood up to greet her. Her piercing eyes suddenly widened. "My God, you're big!" she exclaimed, and walked out.

There were also those who called and were quite polite, calm and willing to talk about both sides of the issue. Some of those who came to the store would walk around looking at items while they talked to me. Some of them would even buy something, as if to acknowledge that I was doing my best to serve my community and, like them, just trying to make a living and raise a family.

The hours of City Council duties kept me away from home, a lot. For Christmas one year, Mardele gave me one of the first cell phones, a Motorola about the size of a brick. I really appreciated that gift, but I also understood the sad rationale behind it. From then on, at least I could call her as I ran from one event or meeting to another.

As I settled into being a councillor, I became increasingly frustrated with those who obviously had not spent the required time

I'm about substance not symbolism.

to study an issue. Rather than engaging in constructive, informed debate, they just ad-libbed whatever they felt at the moment. I saw Council meetings becoming increasingly disjointed and tedious because of it.

Compared to the 1994 Civic Election, the 1997 Election was practically issue-free, as you could tell by the very poor electoral turnout: only half of the voters from 1994 bothered to cast their ballot. My campaign was relatively low-key and I was easily re-elected, as were Mayor Dayday and all of the incumbents except for Ward 8, which was won by Howard Harding, and Ward 1, which elected Jim Madden.

The 2000 Saskatoon civic election was also relatively uneventful, with unimpressive voter interest once again. It was particularly easy for me, as I was acclaimed. My total expenses for the campaign, including brochures, was $1,000. I still stood on the street corners with a placard during the campaign, though this time it simply read,

"Thank you!" My total donations, from both business and non-business, was $1,200.

The biggest news from the election was the embarrassing defeat of Dayday, who ended up finishing third behind Birkmaier and the winning candidate, Jim Madden. The new faces on Council were Lenore Swysten, Owen Fortosky, and Tiffany Paulsen. I was very pleased that former councillor Glen Penner had returned. I admired Councillor Penner's calm, confident demeanor. He always came to meetings well-prepared and made sure all the key questions were raised.

My third term on City Council was by far the most contentious and frustrating for me personally. Not only was Council out of control, but our city as a whole was losing its sense of direction. Jim Madden is a very nice man, but I don't think he ever understood his role as mayor. That role is to bring things to a head, to lead Council in effective decision-making. That wasn't happening, and it wasn't good for anyone. As one Councillor put it, "Jim became mayor because he had an axe to grind, and he ground it."

I felt sorry for the city's bureaucrats, who are in charge of carrying out Council's wishes. Most people don't realize the amount of pressure on our city administrators. The elected councillors and mayor are, collectively, their bosses, so even when an administrator wants to do the right thing, he or she might be prevented from doing so because of ambiguity or political gamesmanship going on behind the scenes. So even though no individual city councillor can direct the city's administration, it takes six votes, when something doesn't go right, the bureaucrats get the blame.

The City Council meeting held on Monday, July 18, 2001, pretty well sums up the state of the City of Saskatoon and its City Council. It was about seven months into Mayor Madden's term. According to the records, the meeting started at 7:00 p.m. and carried on until 2:04 a.m. the following day, making it the longest council meeting in Saskatoon's history. The main issues were Police Chief Dave Scott's contract, big box development, and union contracts. It was a gong show, with everyone going off in their own direction and nothing coming to a conclusion. To make this endurance test even more uncomfortable, the air conditioning had been programmed to shut down at midnight. (Councillor Glen Penner had a plane to catch that Tuesday morning. He said he never wanted to be in a meeting that lasted that long again, and was instrumental in establishing a time limit on all future City Council meetings.)

That summer, the mayor would show up at in-camera meetings wearing very casual summer wear. I know the argument why that shouldn't matter, but I cannot and will not bring myself to accept what I consider disrespect for the most important elected position in the largest and most progressive city in the province, a city destined to be one of the greatest in our country. People have often heard me say, "Casual dress; casual thoughts." I was convinced we were going down the wrong path in the running of our city and determination of its future.

In December of 2002, the casino debate raged on in council until 3 a.m. I couldn't disagree when people started referring to Council meetings as a "gong show" – undisciplined and disorganized.

I decided I would run for mayor in 2003.

Announcing Canada's
Craziest Mayor

FOR ANYONE WHO FOLLOWED CIVIC politics, I don't think it came as a surprise that I decided to run for mayor in 2003. I started planning in late 2002, meeting with a small group that would become my campaign team, and early in the new year, I took advantage of any speaking engagement to promote my vision for the city.

I officially announced my candidacy just before the long weekend in May 2003. The Tuesday after the long weekend, I was back to my tried-and-true Burma Shave strategy, standing on the corner during the morning

You can't move forward when you keep looking in the rear-view mirror.

drive time, waving at passersby. This time, though, I had to cover the city, so from Monday to Friday, from May until election day, I would be out there somewhere in a high traffic zone. One of my favourite locations was on Warman Road near 33rd Street. I remember one of the residents coming out to thank me for helping to slow down traffic – because drivers thought I was a police officer, pulling over drivers.

I remember one commuter in particular. Every day, he would drive by, honk, and then give me the finger. I would smile and give him my very best five roses hand signal in return. (A "five roses" hand signal is an open palm with all five fingers extended.)

One day, he only honked and waved his hand. I guess he got tired of the finger symbol and now would just honk and wave his hand as if to say, "Forget it!" Finally, he gave up honking, too, and just drove by. At that point, I put him down as a "maybe" among my possible supporters.

Running for mayor is a different ball game than running to be a councillor for your ward, especially if you were considered, as I was, a strong contender for the city's top job. You attract considerably more media attention, you're expected to attend all town hall debates, and you have to know what you're talking about on a multitude of wide-ranging issues. My campaign speech notes were 27 pages long.

I decided early on to focus on where the city should be headed — not on where it had been. I wanted to represent the voice of reason, to be seen as someone who could pull disparate sides together, to unite our city in a mood of optimism and purpose. Certainly, the race had become contentious, especially regarding the issue of a possible downtown casino.

Just as importantly, though, our Council and city administration had become mired in bureaucratic bottlenecks and labour issues that were close to the boiling point. We needed direction, and I wanted to provide it. I would start my speeches with, "Saskatoon is the economic generator for the province. In order for our city to be a leader, we must have a vision for the future of our community."

> We must not think about the next election ... but the next generation.

Someone once pointed out to me that I'm not so much a businessman as a salesman, and I'm proud to agree with that assessment. I was frustrated with the lack of salesmanship shown by my predecessors. I wanted to promote Saskatoon to the country and to the world, but most of all to our own citizens. I wanted people to buy into what we had to offer and our promise for the future.

My key topics were development of our downtown (building "up" instead of just "out"); improved policing methods including more patrols, especially foot patrols; better relationships with the unions serving our city; new housing developments that would blur the lines between neighbourhoods, especially between Riversdale and the downtown; and improved transportation in all sectors, notably the need for two new bridges to make our "Circle Drive" truly a circle.

I made myself very clear on current issues. I was not in favour of having a downtown casino. I was dead-set against a proposal to turn a section of our north industrial area into a red-light district. For safety and business reasons, I wanted to move the downtown transit mall. The transit mall was where all the city buses converged for the purposes of transferring from one bus route to another. The area had become unsafe and the subsequent effects

> Culture is how employees' hearts and stomachs feel about Monday morning … on Sunday night.

were devastating for businesses in the surrounding area. I was in favour of economic issues such as big box store developments like Preston Crossing and deconstruction of the Gathercole building. The building had once housed a technical high school and more recently the headquarters for the Saskatoon Public School. It was in poor condition and would have cost a fortune to repair. (It was a great site for development and in fact, in time, became River Landing.)

Running against me was the incumbent, Jim Madden; Louise Carroll; controversial former MP Jim Pankiw; Javed Syed; and Peter Zakreski, a former city councillor. Those mayoralty forums became very heated at times and, unfortunately, turned personal.

Star Phoenix reporter Gerry Klein wrote an article titled, "Election interest at fever pitch." Klein was right;

the election on October 22nd brought out long lines of voters, with the *Star Phoenix* reporting that some polling stations ran out of ballots. One of the big reasons was the plebiscite on the casino, but certainly voters in Saskatoon were once again in favour of change. Fortunately for me, the kind of change I was advocating was the kind of change they wanted. I won the mayoralty with a margin of almost 4,000 votes over Peter Zakreski; Pankiw came in third; and it had to be very disappointing for Jim Madden to come in fourth.

We must teach our children to once again love Saskatoon.

That night is one of the highlights of my life, and I was so glad that my parents were there. But it was also tinged with a bit of sadness and guilt. My father came up to me at the end of the evening and said, "Well, son. Now that you're mayor, you're going to be awfully busy, so I may as well get the keys to the store from you." I put my hand in my pocket, took the keys off the ring, and handed them to him. He then put his hand on my shoulder and said, "I want you to know it's nothing personal; it's just business." He was right. Up until then, I had been working at the store six days a week – seven if I had to do inventory on a Sunday. If I was going to be mayor, I was going to be a full-time mayor.

As eager as I was to get going, I had to bide my time between the election and when I was sworn in as mayor. Then, the following morning, a Tuesday, I could truly begin. Those days in between felt like the longest days of my life.

Mayor Madden, however, was in no hurry to give up his position. I was told he stayed in the office the full last day he was in power, leaving only at 6 p.m. that Monday. They had to ask him for his keys. I can now relate to what he might have felt about having to give up his post.

Being the mayor of a city as dynamic as Saskatoon is not a full-time job. It's two full-time jobs! I am very much a person who likes things to be in order, and who sticks to a routine as much as possible. Typically, my day would begin either by getting into the office by 8 a.m. or attending some function. Regardless, Carol Purich – my trusted assistant and an absolutely amazing, dedicated individual – would

> Being a leader doesn't mean you sail just in calm waters.

be there by 8 a.m. and was often there late into the evening or took her work home with her. Each day, she would be the first person I would talk to. We would discuss the previous day and the day ahead. Although Carol would always have a list of items for discussion, she was also wonderful as a sounding board. Being able to voice aloud my ideas and solutions to a trusted colleague helped me clarify my thoughts.

Carol had the same professional relationship with the three mayors who preceded me (Wright, Dayday, and Madden), although I liked to say she worked for them but worked with me. I truly regarded her as a trusted colleague and relied on her to field inquiries, manage the others who came onto our team, and keep things running smoothly, including meeting arrangements and matters of protocol. Carol was with me from my first day until 2015, when she retired. That entire time, she shared my determination to uphold the duties, the dignity, and the high standards of the Mayor's Office. She deserves our city's thanks.

The corporate culture of the Mayor's Office changed with the beginning of my term – an immediate and permanent change. Before 2003, there wasn't the same level of expectation of loyalty to the mayor – of being part of the mayor's team. But the time had come when that loyalty had to be there, to protect the confidentiality of the office. Unfortunately, the down side to this shift was that when a new mayor was elected, he or she wanted to bring in their own team. In other words, the days of senior staff continuing on in their role in the Mayor's Office from one mayor to the next was over.

People who work for the mayor now have to agree with the mayor. If you don't believe in what the mayor is doing, then you shouldn't be there. (Remember that the Mayor's Office and Administration are separate entities.) I wanted the Mayor's Office to be able to deliver on the promises that I campaigned on. I needed a strong, trustworthy team at arm's length from City Hall bureaucracy in order to do that.

It's difficult for some people to realize that compared to head offices of major corporations – and the City had

3,000 employees – the Mayor's Office had virtually no staff. At first, there was just the two of us. We eventually added Shelley Burke, who helped with research and organizing. In 2013, during my last term, we added Richard Brown, a Peabody and six-time Emmy award-winning Canadian journalist, who became essential to the Mayor's Office as Saskatoon became more prominent on the national and international stage. All of us worked very closely together. When it came to actually writing the speeches, though, I did that myself — although some might say I wasn't the greatest at it. Regardless, I found I was very poor at following a script; I preferred to have my own notes and take it from there.

Typically, the mayor of a city deals with civic administration far more than the councillors do, and that was very true in my case. During the day, there would be internal and external meetings. Monday was devoted primarily to meeting with key City administrators prior to the evening's Council meeting — principally the City Manager Phil Richards (and later, City Manager Murray Totland).

At first, I was interested in working only with Phil. I knew some of the city's bureaucrats were less than thrilled when I became mayor, so I had to work at building those relationships. Yes, in my campaign speeches, our city staff heard my promise to "shake things up at City Hall" loud and clear and understandably were concerned with what I exactly meant by that. To allay concerns, I soon got the message out that I was not going to be a mayor who cleaned house. Nor did I want to become a micro-managing dictator, involved in day-to-day management of projects. My role was to oversee City operations as a whole and if there was a mistake or an issue, to resolve it. Just as the city's general managers learned to trust me, I in turn learned to trust and rely on them.

Information and input is invaluable, because even mayors can make bad decisions — and early on, I made a doozy. Buoyed by my election victory, and in an effort to immediately restore more decorum and order for the

> We need to expand the economy, not the government.

Office of the Mayor, I declared that all meetings with me at City Hall had a dress code of business attire, which meant that men should wear a tie.

I can see now why this idea raised such a fuss. It is a great example of good intentions gone wrong. I wasn't trying to be arrogant. I wasn't trying to sell more ties at our family's store. It wasn't about me at all. It was about showing the same respect for the Office of the Mayor and our city that I did. I wanted to show that City Hall was back to doing business properly, and that meant looking the part. What happened was that many people took this directive as a signal that I was "elitist and corporate" and not interested in having "the common folk" in my office. That was certainly not the case. I quickly saw the error of my decision and reversed it on the same day.

Unfortunately, comedian Rick Mercer and his staff were always on the lookout for Canadian politicians they could lampoon, and this was right up their alley. The next thing I knew, Mercer christened me "Canada's Craziest Mayor." His producers were calling me. I didn't know what to do. Thank goodness Chris Dekker, who managed the City's public affairs, knew exactly what to do: make the most of it! Return the calls! Play along! That way, I owned up to my mistake, and got to laugh with those who were laughing at me. After all, I had been called much worse while wearing goaltender's pads instead of a business suit. (A few years later, I met Rick. I guess everyone makes mistakes in judgement. Mercer said he got serious flack about those "crazy" mayor episodes from people who were concerned about the stigma of mental illness — that being "crazy" was nothing to joke about.)

As much as I got along with a great team of civic administrators and project managers, I did not want to see us expanding our "empire" at City Hall and taking more and more responsibilities in-house. I preferred that we out-source projects that were not within our core competencies. One outcome in doing so is that you then make others with more experience and skills accountable. Secondly, if there is a downturn, the City is not faced with laying off people who have come to rely on us for jobs to pay for their mortgage and raise their children. People who have never had to dismiss an employee, for

A growing city can't be timid.

whatever reason, might think, "Why not bring it in-house into City Hall? Think of the money we'll save!" They make the mistake of thinking that hiring, managing, and keeping the right people is easy. Bringing on more staff can be a big and very costly mistake to make with taxpayer dollars.

Tuesday mornings were my "media mornings," especially with CKOM and Brent Loucks. I was the first mayor to schedule a weekly on-air interview, where I would talk about what had happened at the City Council meeting the evening before. In 13 years, I never missed one of those regular Tuesday

> I'm for job creation … not process creation.

interviews, even if it meant calling from my cell phone in a different time zone halfway around the world. We did the interviews in planes, trains, buses, and cars and from almost every province in Canada. (I distinctly remember one interview when I had to excuse myself from lunch in Dublin with Mardele and Kevin Vickers, at the time the Canadian Ambassador to Ireland, to do my weekly Tuesday media spot.)

The remainder of the weekdays would be spent taking phone calls, meeting with various representatives, and attending the many different committee meetings. I took particularly delight in personally calling back citizens who had contacted the Mayor's Office. They were often surprised that I would do that. You can imagine how totally surprised some of them were when I showed up at their doorstep to talk to them.

I made a point of having regular monthly meetings, usually on a Thursday or Friday, with the president of the University of Saskatchewan. What's good for the University is good for Saskatoon, and vice-versa. Our university – and the more than 22,000 students it brings to campus every fall – has a major impact on our city in many diverse ways, but for too long, there had been too much of a separation between "town and gown" and I wanted us to come together, to work together whenever we could. There is no better an example of the good that can come of that working together than the Canadian Light Source Synchrotron.

The weekends could be even busier than the rest of the week. If there was not a special event, I would go to the Farmers' Market every Saturday, just to talk to people about what was happening in Saskatoon. It was better than any poll, as far as I was concerned, to get a read on what people were thinking and feeling.

Becoming mayor is not a good idea for anyone watching their waistline. In addition to all the breakfasts, there were the luncheons, receptions, and dinners. I would try, albeit not all that successfully, to reserve Wednesdays for lunch with Mardele, just to catch up on things at home, but it would not be unusual for my week to include four breakfasts, five luncheons, ten receptions, and three or four banquets! That, combined with presentations at service clubs, conferences, and conventions going on in Saskatoon, there was never a shortage of a "free lunch."

I was sometimes asked how these dinners and lunches were paid for. Most of the time, it was the accepted practice that whomever asked for the meeting paid for the meal. Not once, though, did I ever expense alcohol to the City. I didn't drink, but if I did buy someone else a glass of wine or a beer, I paid for it myself.

In contrast, one of the healthiest events I ever attended was the Mayor's Marathon to repair the Meewasin Valley Authority trail system. Thanks to 18 months of personal training beforehand, I completed two ultra-marathons – each 55 km in length – in 2014 and 2015.

Most days, the list of events carried on into the evening. Monday night, of course, was the City Council meeting. The rest of the week was filled with dozens of special occasions where my presence was requested and expected. A typical schedule from my calendar shows a new business open house at 4 p.m., followed by a media sponsor night at Prairieland Park at 5 p.m., followed by the Hiroshima/Nagasaki Peace Day event at Rotary Park, followed by a powwow at Dakota Dunes at 7 p.m. I became very familiar with every hall in Saskatoon. I was such a frequent visitor that the staff at TCU Place would bring me my Coca-Cola™ (the symbol of freedom!) without me even asking, and a herbal tea for Mardele if she was joining me.

According to my lose calculation, as mayor, I attended upwards of 20 functions a week, with the heaviest schedules from September through June. Every event was obviously important to the people holding it and I was honoured to be invited. (I kept the invitations to these events.)

I didn't care how large or "visible" the event was. If I could attend, I would. If I couldn't, I would send one of our councillors to represent the city.

When I arrived home, usually around 9 p.m., my day still wasn't over. I would walk the dogs – our two golden retrievers – and then settle down to read the local newspapers (hardcopy and online) from across Canada. In all, there were 17 dailies that I would skim through, starting with the St. John's newspaper and working my way west: Halifax, Montreal, Ottawa, Brampton, London, Mississauga, Hamilton, Windsor, Kitchener-Waterloo, Winnipeg, Edmonton, Calgary, Vancouver, and Surrey.

I found that skimming these papers was a good way to identify what Saskatoon had in common with other major cities, as well as possible situations that might arise in Saskatoon that would need to be addressed. I would send some of these news items off to our top civic administrators such as City Manager Murray Totland, Randy Grauer (Community Services Manager), Jeff Jorgensen (Transportation Manager), or Alan Wallace (Chief Planner) with a note such as: *Could this ever happen here?* or *Notice how they solved this issue.* I wasn't trying to interfere, and I never sent anything to anyone other than our top executive. Rather, I was hoping that I could inspire them to think in new ways, explore different approaches, and also be more prepared for any eventuality in a city of our size.

As for our own newspaper, the *Star Phoenix*, I called them the "word police" – always ready to trip me up or, better yet I suppose, report on where I had stumbled on my own. I remember calling them one time to say I was completely misrepresented because when they quoted me, they omitted the last part of my quote! Their response was, "I guess we were running out of room so we edited that part out."

Sometimes, the reporting seemed malicious. There was an incident where a woman driving on Circle Drive on a winter's day lost control of her vehicle and, because of the snow piled against the guard rail, her car went over the railing and plummeted onto the river ice below. Certainly, a horrific experience, but thankfully she survived. When the media contacted me about the incident, with the angle that proper maintenance of the road would have prevented the driver from going off the

> Facts may hurt your feelings but for some their feelings are their facts, regardless of whether they are true or not.

bridge, I answered their questions thoroughly. As an afterthought, I cautioned motorists everywhere throughout the city to be careful because of the very icy conditions. Later that evening, the story came out to the effect of "Mayor blames motorist for accident on Circle Drive Bridge."

Although I was often frustrated by this incomplete

or biased journalistic perspective, I don't perceive the media as "fake." I appreciate how journalists are essential to keeping governments in line. Thanks to their watchfulness, I can at least rely on the published accounts of our city's journalists for proof that I was never involved in any scandals or grey area issues involving ethics. I was always very sure to make sure all my expense accounts, and all my dealings with everyone, were completely transparent and proper.

Along with the scrutiny from hard-nosed editorial writers, the mayor's job comes with an ample number of other critics. Here, I must make special mention of the Raging Grannies (a group of women who protest to promote peace, justice, and equality through humour and song), who one day invaded the main reception area of City Hall, singing protest songs at the top of their lungs. Did I go down to meet them? No. It wasn't that I didn't respect their right to protest; good for them on that count. It was the fact that as a mayor you always have to remember that you represent all voters, and at that moment I was engaged with another matter that was important to other good-hearted, hard-working taxpayers in our community. If all you did was react to negative comments in this job, you would never get anything done, nor would you have the information to have the accurate, big picture required to make the best decisions. If you waited until you were sure you pleased everyone, you would never come to any decision, and if you did, somebody would still complain.

Complaints and protests are one thing. Threats are another. One incident early in my first term affected me to the core. Mardele and I were at a late afternoon Remembrance Day event on November 11, 2003 at the Army, Navy and Veterans (ANAVETS) Hall. It was one of my first events as a mayor, and I was so pleased to be there to represent the city. At the end of the program, I was moving around the crowd, shaking hands and exchanging pleasantries, when this younger man in uniform came right up to my face. "If I had a gun right now, I would shoot you," he said. It wasn't just the way he said it, but the look in his eyes that immediately chilled me to the bone. There was not the least doubt in my mind, nor would it be in the mind of anyone who experienced a similar situation: this was a death threat. I immediately found Mardele and said, "Let's go. We're out of here."

I immediately called Dan Wiks, our Deputy Chief of Police, who happened to be driving home from Edmonton. He told us to get to a public place immediately and he would meet us there as soon as he got into town. Mardele and I went to the Station Place Restaurant and waited for him. Soon after, Wiks arrived and we discussed our safety and the safety of our family, and the security of our home.

As unnerving as that incident was, I kept it private, and in the end it strengthened my resolve to be a mayor who would not be bullied into being silent or stray from my mission. As I was also to learn, this would not be an isolated incident. Over my years as mayor, I learned that physical threats to public officials are far more common than people realize.

You cannot help but be jarred by a menacing message in the mail or on your phone when you come into work in the morning. The threats were invariably vague, rather than pinpointing a particular issue. I felt sorry for our staff, who were on the front line for much of this. For one of our staff, these messages almost drove her to quit her job. I won't say I just took the vitriol in stride, but I did try to put it into perspective.

In spite of the lack of a specific threat, we remained vigilant. When I was away, the police would check up on Mardele and there were some nights when she left the lights on. I made it a practice of not publishing my full daily itinerary in advance – a practice other aspiring city councillors and mayors should note.

The threats were most common during my first term, then dwindled as time went on. Maybe it was because some of these callers thought they could get me to quit, and then gave up. Another reason, I think, was that technology was making it increasingly easy to trace calls. Thankfully, only that ANAVETS incident brought me within reach of someone who threatened to harm me or my family. Compared to some other elected officials I have known, I have been lucky.

Tomorrow's News

DURING ONE OF HIS SEVERAL VISITS TO Saskatoon, I asked a visiting consul general from a Pacific Rim country why he and many investors from places like Singapore, Taiwan, the Philippines, and China were so interested in Saskatoon. He replied, "In Canada, Toronto is yesterday's news, Calgary is today's news, and Saskatoon is tomorrow's news."

I think he's right. I was fortunate to have been mayor during a time in our city's history which Professor Joe Garcia, a University of Saskatchewan political studies professor and frequent political commentator, called an era "of substantial development." City Councillor Mairin Loewen described this 13-year period as "a shift in Saskatoon's size and attitude." I believe it will be known as a time when Saskatoon grew from being one of many communities in Saskatchewan to an emerging city state which, although part of the province, has its own distinct economy, culture and potential; similar to the type of relationship of Toronto to Ontario, or New York City to the state of New York. The completion of the South Bridge, which finally made our Circle Drive a true circle, was a symbol of our transition to a major urban centre.

It would be ridiculous to say I was the one who created a boom in the resource sector, brought about sufficient rain for agriculture, and the myriad of other interrelated factors that led to this significant period in Saskatoon's history. (It was Alberta premier Ed Stelmach who raised the resource royalties in his province that prompted drilling companies to concentrate their operations in Saskatchewan.) I did appreciate the sentiment, though, of *Saskatchewan Chinese Entrepreneur* magazine, who called me, "The patron saint of Saskatoon" and described me as one who "serves as guardian and protector for its future."

In every one of my campaigns for mayor, I would be asked about my ambitious plans for Saskatoon and what I was promising. My answer was always, "I'm going to work as hard as possible to

When given the opportunity to lead, lead.

make Saskatoon better than it is today. That is my only promise. The rest are all goals." In the City of Saskatoon, the mayor only has one vote and decisions are made through consensus. This is different than some other jurisdictions in Canada, particularly in Ontario, where the mayor has more significant powers, including vetoing council decisions. So the Saskatoon city system works on a "consensus mayor" structure not a "strong mayor" structure Thus, I worked as hard as I could to make sure we did not squander the opportunities that providence had bestowed upon our city during my four terms as mayor. As far as I'm concerned, I lived up to that promise every day.

I will readily admit to the accusation – from the media, general public, and even within city administration – that I'm a big thinker or even that I think too big. Frankly, I don't have much time for leaders, elected or otherwise, who cannot or will not lift their eyes to the far horizon, and are only led by the polls.

I have been outright ridiculed for suggesting we enclose an area of downtown in a climate-controlled atrium, which would cover from the Delta Bessborough Hotel to the Midtown Plaza, from 19th Street to 23rd Street. Structures like that are being built in other cities, "but it could never happen here" shouted the naysayers. No doubt there were individuals who thought we were too small in 1907 to have a university, and if we did, it should be built out of cheap lumber. But the provincial leaders did not agree with those small ideas and today the five most prominent of its original buildings have been called "the finest grouping of Collegiate Gothic university buildings in Canada." The original buildings were constructed from

Greystone, a locally-sourced dolomitic limestone and when the local supply of greystone ran out, the university used Tyndall stone from Manitoba. The buildings are decorated with arches, crenellations, buttresses, and bay windows and the university as a whole is known for its beauty and green spaces.

There were also the BANANAs (build absolutely nothing anywhere near anyone). A performing arts and convention centre like TCU Place? No way! Who's going to support that? Or a state-of-the-art hockey arena, or a Field House, or an Olympic swimming pool ... well you get the idea. The fact is, great cities are built on great ideas by people with great confidence and determination – not those who find it much easier to sit and whine, or study a project to death.

Whether you like it or not, Saskatoon is destined to grow. It's how we grow that matters. Fortunately for us we can look at other cities, such as Calgary and Edmonton, for lessons to help guide our own planning. We can learn from our own past mistakes, such as the decisions that led to new neighbourhoods where we perpetuated the 1950's love of the suburb and ignored pedestrians needs.

When I first came onto City Council, I didn't know a thing about urban planning, but by the time I became mayor I had come to realize just how important urban planning is. My most important lesson about urban planning is that a plan should follow the money – and by that, I mean where people want to spend their money on buying a home. It's people who should shape neighbourhoods – not the other way around.

As Saskatoon grows, we also have to understand and become a leader at solving problems that are typical of big cities. I refuse to use the term "inner city" because I don't want any negative reference to any of our neighbourhoods, but that doesn't mean there aren't inequalities that need to be overcome. Saskatoon must face the fact that despite our growth, or even in some cases because of it, we need to do a better job of reducing crime and ensuring that all neighbourhoods are safe, healthy, and encourage inclusiveness and equality.

My travels as mayor taught me that different cities do different things right. In Singapore, everyone had a home to live in, regardless of income. In Shanghai, all the buildings are different and create a spectacular skyline, especially at night. Berlin has no landfill; they turn all of their waste into energy. As I saw these cities doing things differently, I would ask myself, "Why can't we do that here?"

Money is fluid; it will go to where there is the least resistance, and that's where a good City Council and city administration can play an important role in guiding investment to achieve mutual benefits. For example, if you want your city to go up instead of sprawling outward, then you need to have bylaws and tax structures that attract downtown developers. One of my regrets is that in 2016, City Council approved a bylaw to limit the height of buildings in our downtown. I should have fought harder against that decision. What we should have done is given tax concessions that encouraged builders to go even higher. For that matter, why not allow tall buildings in suburbs? Think of the farmland that could be saved!

Generally, though, city administration and City Council paid attention to what the private sector was telling us and we were willing to be competitive in attracting good companies and developers. My first priority, always, was to see what was best for all Saskatoon residents, and what I found more often than not was that you could indeed have the best of both worlds – public and private.

> Some believe in government dependence; I believe in financial independence

For example, when Regina put in stiff zoning regulations for their suburbs, Saskatoon allowed much more leeway. After all, developers have a very good instinct for what the market wants, and are strongly motivated to compete for that market. Why impose needless restrictions on that process? For that reason, we began to attract developers away from Regina and into our city. We created the new neighbourhoods of Silverspring, Willowgrove, Erindale, Evergreen, Arbor Creek, Aspen Ridge, Rosewood, University Heights, Blairmore, Hampton Village, and Holmwood. I would be happy to live in any of these neighbourhoods, just as much as I would in any of our well-established ones.

From my first day as mayor, I could sense that

Saskatoon was on the threshold of a new era, and thankfully there were others who shared that view. One barometer of optimism, I believe, was how close we came to a change in provincial government in 2003, the same year I was elected mayor. Four years later in the 2007 provincial election, the overwhelming victory of the Saskatchewan Party confirmed that, right or wrong, the people of Saskatchewan wanted something new, and had adopted a more entrepreneurial, optimistic spirit.

I began to notice a change in attitude toward our province — and Saskatoon in particular — from beyond our provincial and even national borders. I remember the first Big City Mayors (BCM) conference I attended, held in 2004 in Gatineau, Quebec. These conferences were held three or four times a year, and included 22 cities from across Canada. At the 2004 conference, I felt like the weak sister, especially compared to Pat Fiacco, Mayor of Regina, who was much better connected than I was. I didn't say too much at that conference, but I felt compelled to go up to David Miller, Mayor of Toronto and an obvious leader among the group, *Words inspire and actions create change.* to point out to him why I felt Saskatoon deserved to be at the table. We weren't a capital city, I said, but we were our province's largest city, the economic generator, and the hub of major provincial and western Canadian activity. As I walked away, I overheard Miller ask one of his staffers for "the file on Saskatoon." I made note of that, and from then on built up my own files to be better attuned to what was going on in other Canadian urban centres.

Each time I attended a BCM conference, I noticed a growing change in attitude toward Saskatoon. We were the city getting positive attention in the press, and were becoming national leaders according to several key economic indicators. By my third and fourth terms as mayor, Saskatoon was no longer a wallflower at these conferences; we were at times the centre of attention.

We were receiving attention much farther afield, too. I began to get calls from overseas and the USA. Exploratory delegations were now coming here. The Mayor's Office didn't have a budget for a press clipping service, though, so I had no way of tracking how much was actually reported about Saskatoon nationally or internationally.

We were also getting calls from the banks. Bragging about your city is one thing, but if you really want to know what people think of your brilliant idea, or venture, or your city, ask them for money. Better yet, wait and see how many of them come to you, asking if you'll take their money! That was the case for Saskatoon. We had a triple-A rating, the highest rating there is. We earned it through balanced assets and debt, along with significant investment in infrastructure that would serve us well into the future. We had the banks and other financial heavyweights calling us, wanting to sell debentures because they had clients eager to invest in us.

Certainly, there were those who argued that we

should not take the money, that we should just sit on our hands and do nothing, but it is important to be ready to answer the door when opportunity knocks, and especially when it bangs. I could name a hundred cities that would have loved to have had our credit rating with Standard and Poor's, and would gladly have found ways to invest in major projects for the good of their citizens now and for decades to come. I have no doubt that we leveraged our position to our best advantage. Proof of that, in part, is that we maintained a superior credit rating the entire time that I was mayor.

Our major promoters, the Saskatoon Regional Economic Development Authority (SREDA) and Tourism Saskatoon (now called Discover Saskatoon), were enjoying considerable success in opening doors and attracting interest. At the same time, I visited cities in Asia and Europe to promote our city and develop ties to international investors. Our provincial government did its part by promoting the province, and once anyone became interested in Saskatchewan, they would almost invariably take an interest in its most dynamic city.

We were fortunate to have individuals and corporations from Saskatoon who were great boosters. Bill Doyle, who became CEO of PotashCorp in 1999, was someone who deserves more credit than he's been given for his contribution to our city's economy and reputation. PotashCorp (now Nutrien) completed a billion-dollar expansion just as Saskatoon's economy was beginning to take off.

Bill and I would try to meet on a quarterly basis to talk about Saskatoon and any concerns he had about the city. We would often meet at John's Restaurant for lunch or supper and occasionally I would go to Bill's office. At one meeting, he asked me, "Well, your worship, what do you want today?"

I replied, "I can't believe you would ask that."

Bill responded, "You always want something."

"Well, I need a new bridge," I said, thinking about the Victoria Bridge (or Traffic Bridge as it is now known).

At his raised eyebrow, I continued, "What else? How about a new art gallery? Or a new playground?

Bill asked, "Where and how much?"

I responded, "Kinsmen Park. As much as $10M."

"Leave it with me," he said.

I received a phone call from Bill a few weeks later. He said, "Well, your worship, I'll look after the redevelopment of Kinsmen Park but I can only announce $5M. But, I'm good for the rest."

As the project progressed, it was going over budget and the administration was wanting to cut back on the plans. I said, "Leave it with me." I phoned Bill and he gave us another $2.5M to complete the project. Later, I spoke with Bill and said I really need a new train for the children, especially for those with special needs. The train was a replica modern-day freight train that rolled along a 626-metre loop through the park. I saw how parents had to struggle to get their children onto the train, it was painful for everyone.

Bill said, "Leave it with me." Canpotex came to the table for the railcars. If you look closely you will see they are exactly the same as a real Canpotex potash car; convex not straight with real running numbers on the side of the cars – just like the Canpotex fleet. A few weeks later, I was asked to a lunch with Bill, Steven Dechka (President of Canpotex) and Fred Green (President of CP Rail). As we were having lunch, Bill mentioned to Fred that a refurbishing of Kinsmen Park was underway and we needed an engine for the train. "Don't you think you would like to help the mayor?"

Fred paused for a minute and said, "Okay, okay, I'll buy the mayor his engine." I told Fred the engine will be an exact replica of a CP Rail engine to the smallest detail. (The replica engine has its own running number as part of the CP Rail fleet. If you go to the CP website and type in the number of the engine, it will tell you that it is sitting in Saskatoon.)

It's people like Bill and Steve who have made a substantial contribution to Saskatoon and that is why it is so important to have international and nation headquarters in one's community. They make a difference. The park is now called Nutrien Playland at Kinsmen Park.

Kent Smith-Windsor, who was Executive Director of the Greater Saskatoon Chamber of Commerce throughout my terms as mayor, pushed our Council to pass a motion during my first term as mayor, pronouncing a goal to make Saskatoon "Canada's most business-friendly city." There were many other ambassadors I could add to this list. We had very determined, forward-thinking and well-connected business people in the North Saskatoon Business Association, headed by their indomitable executive director, Shirley Ryan. Everywhere our ambassadors from a multitude of industries and sectors went, on all those conferences and conventions, they extolled the advantages of Saskatoon as a place to build a business and raise a family, and were living proof that we were a place of justified optimism.

During those times, how could you not feel excited about Saskatoon? I was dead serious about making the most of our good fortune, and played my role as best I could. For example, when the meat-processing giant Olymel, which exports to over 65 countries, expressed interest in Saskatoon, I flew out to their head office in St. Hyacinthe, Quebec to meet with them, then flew back the same day.

It's not just the successes that deserve our praise. Sometimes even failed attempts can still yield positive results. I will always remember the tremendous amount of work that Murray Osborne, Bill Peterson, and Peter Zakreski put into the city's 2002 bid for the 2007 Summer World University Games. Not getting the Games was one of my biggest disappointments as a City Councillor. At the same time, the fact that we were a finalist showed our country and the world, once again, that we were for real. We were the Canadian competitor against cities like Rome, Mexico City, and Moscow. We were in the big leagues, which was an accomplishment in itself. (In our bid, we made promises of what facilities we would build or improve. During my time as mayor, everything we said we would do in our bid as far as facilities were concerned, we accomplished.)

Inside City Hall, I urged the city's administrative leaders to share my big-picture vision and prepare for it. When they started discussing the eventuality of Saskatoon reaching a population of 250,000, I would ask them to think of a city of a million. Generally, I would not sign off on planning unless it was for a population of 500,000 or more. I asked Theresa Dust, our city solicitor, to imagine the day when our surrounding communities of Corman Park, Osler, Warman, and Martensville would become part of Saskatoon. We even held several consultations, involving 13 Saskatchewan cities and Rural Municipalities (RMs), to discuss our relationships and how they might evolve.

I never regarded this period of substantial growth as a "boom." I dislike the word because it implies an inevitable bust. Saskatoon will certainly have its ups and downs economically, but there's nothing that should stop us from being a consistent provincial —and national — leader in service and manufacturing, arts and culture, sports, quality of life, education, and research. The opportunities are there for us to leverage, or to squander.

With my involvement in sports, especially hockey,

people have often asked me about the possibility of bringing a professional hockey or football team to Saskatoon. I'm certain it will happen, but so far, the timing has not seemed right. As far as a CFL team is concerned, I think it's realistic for Saskatchewan to have two pro football teams just like Alberta. When the Stampeders joined the CFL in 1945, Calgary's population was just over 97,000; when the Eskimos joined in 1949, Edmonton's population was roughly 137,000 – a combined total population that is less than that of greater Saskatoon now. I remember making a remark to that effect to CFL Commissioner Jeffrey Orridge at an event in Saskatoon several years ago. He turned his back on me and never spoke to me again. Call it an incomplete pass, but the game's far from over.

River Landing

IN WESTERN CANADA, GROWTH HAS historically been synonymous with sprawl. Unfortunately, sprawl and its suburb mentality often leads to downtowns that either become concrete commercial centers that lose all sign of life after business hours or are left to deteriorate with problems nobody is willing to solve.

In my first *State of the City Address* (December of 2003), I stressed that the city centre was going to be a priority of City Council and City Hall. My reason was simple. I said, "If there is no heart, there is no city." I set a goal of 10,000 people living downtown – the equivalent population of two-and-a-half suburban neighbourhoods such as Lakeview.

There was no question where we should start.

The same place where civilizations typically start: at the water's edge.

Long before the arrival of John Lake and his Temperance Colony in 1882 to the area known Nutana, the South Saskatchewan River had been a major route for Indigenous Peoples and the early fur traders. As settlement and trade increased, there were those who envisioned a Mississippi of the north, with Saskatoon being a major city along this proposed trade route. The South Saskatchewan, though, proved far too unpredictable, with fluctuating water levels, treacherous currents, and sandbars that could shift overnight. The wreck of the steamboat "City of Medicine Hat" at the old Traffic Bridge in 1907, along with the development of the more efficient and dependable railway, signalled the end of commercial transportation on the river.

Despite the natural beauty of our river valley, the river itself has never been suitable for most types of recreation. The reasons are the same as they were for commercial purposes. You can never predict from one day to the next what the river will do. Those who are lured to the river during its lower periods in summer love the sand and the cooling water — but in an instant, tragedy can – and does – happen.

Thus, for decades our focus had been not on using the river, but getting over it. We became the "Paris of the Prairies" and "City of Bridges." Along with the bridges we still needed to build, though, were bridges between cultures and communities. When I thought back to the East Side vs West Side hockey game I played in so long ago, it was the river that divided us. I wanted a place where the river would unite us as a community, and physically link the neighbourhoods of Broadway, downtown, and Riversdale.

True, we had built magnificent churches, major hotels, and impressive homes along the river. The Province of Saskatchewan established the Meewasin Valley Authority in 1979 – governed by a 12-member board representing the City, the University of Saskatchewan, and the province — to preserve the river valley's natural beauty and cultural heritage, and to encourage sustainable recreational use of the riverbank. But we could never figure out how to truly leverage the natural attraction of the waterway when it came to the downtown riverbank area between the old Traffic Bridge and the Senator Sid Buckwold Bridge (Idylwyld Drive). That's where I wanted to focus, and in particular on the land which became known as River Landing Phase I, previously called Parcel Y, on the site of what used to be the Technical Collegiate.

In 1992, Mayor Henry Dayday was quoted as saying, "There's absolutely no way Saskatoon taxpayers can afford to put $3 million towards construction of a city centre," in reference to a project proposal involving various levels of government. To my way of thinking, we could never afford not to ensure a vibrant city centre. Dayday's pronouncement came at a time – in late November of that year – when the city was starting to get excited about plans to develop a major water-related tourism attraction.

At the time, Fred Heal, executive director of the Meewasin Valley Authority brought in Ernst & Young as a partnership to drive what was called River Center. It attracted significant interest, especially from our leaders in tourism and economic development. A delegation of 34 led by the Greater Saskatoon Chamber of Commerce and Tourism Saskatoon visited Chattanooga to view the Tennessee Aquarium. But the numbers didn't work. As seemed to happen repeatedly, the dreams never amounted to anything.

As a city councillor, I became particularly enthused with a proposal from Bob Anderson, Betty Anne Latrace-Henderson, and Mike and Howie Stensrud from Miners Construction. They had what I thought was a very viable plan to transform the Gathercole Centre (or what I preferred to call "the old Tech") into a spa hotel. I worked hard to support them, all the while being careful not to cross the line. (At no time while in public office did I ever have any personal investments in any of the projects in our city, anywhere.) Unfortunately, the spa hotel idea was rejected by Council, many of whom had a "my way or no way" attitude and wanted something much more modest – make that mundane – for the site.

I was determined that in my term as mayor we would finally accomplish an impressive transformation of what had become – despite all the rhetoric for more than a quarter-century – a snow dump area and abandoned building.

To say my enthusiasm was pent-up would be an understatement. During all three terms as city councillor, I had hoped we could get something going, but to no avail. Mayor Dayday kept referring to possible development of Block 146, a vacant lot north of 19th Street. I kept insisting to him that Block 146 would never get developed until we first developed the riverfront. One day, he asked in frustration "What are you? Some kind of soothsayer?"

As it turned out, I was.

Parcel Y symbolized to me what we needed to change in Saskatoon. It had become a dead end, not only in our development but also in our thinking. As a councillor, I had come to see Saskatoon as a city in disarray. I wanted to show people that change can be good, that we could achieve excellence. River Landing to me would make the statement that we could overcome our frustration with what *was* wrong with Saskatoon, even though it was hard to know exactly what was wrong. To me, though, the *symbol* of what was wrong was the Gathercole building. In spite of some very vocal supporters, the building was standing in the way of progress — both literally and symbolically. I saw nothing in the building, especially its history, that I wanted to preserve.

Prior to the construction of this building in 1931, Parcel Y had been Saskatoon's Chinatown, which had its beginnings with the coming of the railroad on the west side of the river. The rivalry between Nutana and Saskatoon intensified when the west side development became the Village of Saskatoon in 1901, with the railway station determining once and for all the location of the commercial hub of our future city.

The railway station was situated at what is now Midtown Plaza. Riversdale and other parts of the downtown were being developed by primarily Caucasian entrepreneurs. Chinese immigrants to Saskatoon started developing Parcel Y with their various businesses, turning it into Saskatoon's Chinatown. Whether or not we like to admit it, the majority of Caucasian citizens at that time on both sides of the river were suspicious of Chinatown and wanted to see it disappear. To quote Jeff O'Brien, local historian and City of Saskatoon archivist, Saskatoon's Chinatown was "widely rumoured to be a haven for crime and vice."

The rumours about Chinatown were largely unsubstantiated. As a group, these newcomers to Canada were trying to make a new start in a new land — the same goal as their neighbours from other countries. Regardless of this reality, in the 1920s, the City began to acquire the land in stages so that by the end of the decade the Chinese businesses and residents were completely displaced. The outcome of this movement created a new concern: residents of the surrounding neighbourhoods became worried about devaluation of their property when many of the Chinese did not leave Saskatoon but chose instead to re-establish themselves in the Riversdale neighbourhood.

From today's perspective, I admire the tenacity of these early Asian citizens of Saskatoon who made their own significant contribution to the development of our city. I am pleased that the logo City Council approved for River Landing has design elements acknowledging their historical presence on this site.

> We need to respect our past ... but build on it instead of letting it hold us back.

The assembled land was then used by the City to build the Saskatoon Royal Canadian Legion Hall and Saskatoon Technical Collegiate. The Saskatoon Arena was built six years later, in 1937. The "Tech" eventually became Riverside Collegiate, then renamed The F.J. Gathercole Centre to house the offices of the Saskatoon Public School Board. By the time I became mayor, the Public School Board had moved to a new location downtown on 21st Street and 2nd Avenue (previously the Eaton's store), and the Gathercole building was vacant. The area of Parcel Y and the adjacent areas became known as South Downtown.

In 1978, internationally renowned Canadian architect Raymond Moriyama was commissioned to create a master plan for this site. Moriyama had designed major public structures such as the Canadian War Museum and the Ontario Science Centre. I think it is ironic that a man who came from a Japanese family in Vancouver that was forced into an internment camp in World War II was asked to create the plan for this site, given its history.

Moriyama produced *The South Downtown Concept*

which included the Gathercole site along with the adjacent property between the Broadway Bridge and Victoria Park in Riversdale. His plan sought to remove the psychological as well as physical barriers between Riversdale and the downtown, setting the stage for an even broader vision in the future – the Cultural Crescent — which crossed the river to include Broadway.

As I said earlier, it was obvious to me that the Gathercole building was not worth preserving and was standing, literally, in the way of progress. That conclusion, although shared by many, was also strongly opposed by those who saw the building as a symbol of our heritage and interpreted my definition of progress as cold-hearted commercialization and privatization of a communal gathering place. People who had hardly ever been in the building or had frankly never even given it a second thought rallied in defence of its survival. In other words, it became a very political issue, with fervent local social activists clamoring for its preservation.

I remember a meeting held in the city manager's boardroom at City Hall shortly after I became mayor. It was a meeting with City Solicitor Theresa Dust, Doug Zelinski from the provincial government, and Peter Prebble, who was at this time an MLA with the governing NDP party led by Lorne Calvert. Peter was, to nobody's surprise, siding with the group opposed to the new development. He and his colleagues were calling River Landing (which became the new name to replace "South

Downtown Project" and "Gathercole Site") a "rich person's development." I responded by saying that it wasn't just a downtown development, but a project that would bring the three founding communities of downtown, Riversdale and Nutana together. It would be for everyone. After the meeting, Zelinski pulled me aside and said I had "hit a home run" with my argument.

Personally, I don't think it was ever really about the building. It was about the fear of change, and blindly following a dogma that commerce was bad and only evil people tear down buildings. If it were the Bessborough Hotel, I would completely understand. But as one person once remarked to me, "Over the years, there have been hundreds of photos and paintings of the Bessborough and the churches along Spadina Crescent. When have you ever seen a painting of the Gathercole Centre?" If it were a symbol of anything, it was a symbol of mistreatment of a minority group, as far as I was concerned.

Such is the life of a city councillor or mayor. In trying to bring the citizens of Saskatoon together, my advocacy of Moriyama's vision had created a very pronounced divide between the pro- and anti-development factions in our city. But despite all the clamour and pushback, I was determined to get this project moving ahead.

On December 10, 2003 – just a month after becoming mayor – I delivered my first *State of the City Address.* "Monday was the start of a new era," I said. "Your City Council decided to move ahead after waiting 25 years, ten councils, and four mayors. Yes. We finally did it. The Gathercole site project is under way. We are going to be a city of doers, not naysayers. We are going to have a river valley that the rest of North America will want to visit."

At that time, we had a $4.5 million commitment from the provincial government, and a pledge from the Meewasin Valley Authority to raise $4 million to develop a river-edge park. All we needed was another $1 million to meet the projected cost.

The night before my *State of the City Address*, we had

New developments are like a goose that keeps laying golden eggs.

completed the largest capital budget in the history of the city: $100 million. Of that, $3.9 million was allocated to development of what we were still calling South Downtown.

As for the Gathercole Building, two different consultants had previously come to the same conclusion: that it should be torn down. Finally, after considerable work, the City owned the property and literally cleared the way for development. In running for mayor for the first time, I saw a real opportunity to create an iconic legacy development in the heart of our city.

In 2004, the completed and updated *South Downtown Concept Plan* clarified the vision. It was approved by City Council in June of that year, and by the Meewasin Valley Authority in October. Things became quite heated during that period. At a Council meeting in early 2004, I informed Council that we were going to come to a final decision about South Downtown, and we were not going to adjourn until things were settled. At that meeting, I had on my desk a pile of reports on South Downtown that administration had assembled for me. The stack was over three feet high. I told all the councillors that if they had any questions, I would look up the answers from the reports, regardless of how long it took.

After hearing from all the scheduled speakers from the general public – and there were many – I called a 15-minute recess. It was a strategic move. Taking a recess was like giving a boxer a chance to recover between rounds, as in "You can do it, champ!" It didn't take long after the recess for Council to give approval for development to proceed, just as I had hoped.

The speakers against development were so vicious that night, they actually generated support for the development. Someone who had watched the proceedings on television told me he hadn't really cared one way or another until he saw how I was being attacked, how emotional and irrational the anti-development argument had become, that he decided to take my side. Speakers at the council meeting accused me of being a thief, a liar, that my next suit should be black and white stripes, that I was just selling out to the big money developers, that I was changing the city for the worse.

Every time somebody suggested I was breaking the law, I would turn to our City Solicitor Theresa Dust for her opinion, and she would assure us that no laws were being broken. I would then just move on. Lenore Swystun, who was no longer on Council, was particularly vocal, although never defamatory or abusive. On South Downtown and other matters she became, if you will, the "leader of the opposition," doing everything possible to delay progress. It was a night to remember, but it was worth it. Council voted to adopt the plan. We could now move forward, once and for all, with no turning back – not on my watch.

The animosity among councillors quickly disappeared after that night, and Council came together with a mutual focus. I will always be grateful for the thousands of hours each of them put into the meetings, the research, the discussions and, yes, the debates! Whatever I asked of them, though, they responded. They understood that the only way we were finally going to do what so many other councils had failed to do was to put in a tremendous amount of energy, and never give up.

On November 1, 2004, Council overwhelmingly (10 to 1) approved the proposed name of "River Landing" and unanimously approved the logo. As Councillor Terry Alm said at the time, "We'll no longer be calling it the A.L. Cole or Gathercole property." He was right. The new name quickly caught on.

Work began on the public space of River Landing. The water park went up. The Farmers' Market opened its doors, as did the incubator offices. At last, Riversdale was connected to the downtown along the riverbank. I did everything I could to speed things along. I even convinced City Manager Phil Richards to install sod instead of grass seed. More than once I would say to Phil, "I'll worry about the money. You just worry about getting the project done."

I liked playing the role of the coach who would tell his team to go big or go home. Chris Dekker came to me one day to talk about plans for the new Farmers' Market building. He said that putting in the windows on the north side of the building would put the project over budget, and suggested we not install them. I replied, "If we were the private sector, would you be putting them in?"

"Absolutely," said Chris.

"Then, if the private sector would do it, we have to do it. We have to follow the same set of rules. Otherwise, having two sets of rules just sets you up for failure."

It wasn't just the River Landing site itself

> When your opponents don't like the subject or are losing, they just stop talking about it.

that was so important to us; it was the whole concept of connecting our East Side and West Side once and for all. How did we end up having a city where, if you crossed the street – Idylwyld Drive – into Riversdale, you entered part of the city that many of our citizens refused to visit? Mardele and I would go to Riversdale almost every week for Chinese food, usually the Golden Dragon, and then the Mandarin when the Dragon closed down. She likes to remind me of the time we were standing at the corner of Avenue C and 20th Street, which was infamous at that time.

We were talking about the neighbourhood – the stores, the housing – and I put my hands on my hips and said, "This could be so great. I can see things happening here. We just need someone to get us there." Mardele says I believed in Riversdale when nobody else did. I'm sure there were others who shared my conviction, but I don't think there were many, at least not then.

I remember representatives from the Farmers' Market addressing council about the plan to move the Market from in front of City Hall to Riversdale. They told us that if we moved the Farmers' Market to Riversdale, "nobody will come." That was an understandable concern at the time. Instead, though, the Farmers' Market flourished in its new River Landing location, proving how the right projects can change not only landscapes, but also minds.

Governments at all levels can do much to spur the confidence of other investors, and I knew that would be true for River Landing. The city's ambitious work on the site played a major role in the ensuing construction of Persephone Theatre – the envy of community theatre companies everywhere – and the office buildings with restaurants. We were very fortunate as a city to have such outstanding city administrators like Phil Richards and Chris Dekker, who went far above and beyond their job descriptions and whose passion for this project was every

> We may be in the same storm, but we are definitely not in the same boat.

bit as strong as my own.

The crown jewel of River Landing is the Remai Modern Art Gallery. I called it a landmark public private partnership in my *2015 State of the City Address.* It's also a great example of how you need to take advantage of opportunities when they arise.

If somebody offered you $700,000 cash so you could buy a million-dollar home for $300,000, would you take the money and buy the home? What if you didn't want a new home? What if you said, "But I'd really like to just take your money and do something else" and they replied, "No, we'll give you this money only if you buy a million-dollar home." Would you then turn down the offer? Of course not. You take

> Think not only what a major project will bring the city in the next few years ... but in the next few decades.

advantage of an ideal situation or attractive offer when you can.

That was the situation with the Remai Modern Art Gallery, an important part of the new development. There was no money on the table for any other type of structure or project. It was the gallery or nothing. We were looking at $105 million from Ellen Remai; $17 million from the province; and $13 million from the federal government. There were also donations through a major campaign, along with Ellen's donation of her collection of 450 Picasso prints. Renovating the old Mendel Art Gallery on Spadina Crescent would have cost the city $31 million and received very little outside funding. For $2 million dollars less of taxpayer money, we built a world-class gallery and public centre five times the size of the Mendel.

The Remai Modern was a bit of an albatross around my neck, and I was discouraged by the fact that the people against the project were so much more vociferous than the many people who supported it. At least some people stopped accusing me of being just a "jock" who wanted to build nothing but hockey rinks, or a "cut-throat businessman" who had no time for cultural matters like the arts.

Ellen Remai and her donations and collections is what made this magnificent gallery possible. It is often considerable donations such as this that create buildings and institutions that last decades, if not centuries. Think of Carnegie Hall, the Smithsonian Institute, and Saskatoon's own Mendel Art Gallery.

Even though the Mendel has served the citizens of Saskatoon well for over half a century, at the time it was being planned in 1963, it received its own share of ridicule and criticism. The Mendel was going to cost $410,000, with Fred Mendel donating $175,000 along with an estimated $100,000 in artwork. Mayor Sid Buckwold played a major role in getting the Mendel built amid the controversy, and in 1988 his efforts were acknowledged by Mayor Cliff Wright with a lifetime membership at the Mendel Gallery.

To those who think our new gallery is a waste of money, I say, "Ask the citizens of Saskatoon a hundred years from now." The new facility is already earned international acclaim, exceeded visitor and revenue expectations in its first year of operation, and is becoming as much-loved as the Mendel has been in the past.

The Remai Modern was important on many fronts, especially how its development lead to other building project commitments. I was told straight-up by the developers of the hotel/condo on River Landing, "No Remai Modern Art Gallery, no us." We were also told, "No bridge, no us." The president of Cineplex said, "If they don't build the new Persephone, we're not building our movie theatre." My point is, developments like River Landing are complex, multi-dimensional, and dependent not only on making the right decisions, but making them at the right time, in the right order. Critics tend to see things from only a limited, single perspective. Any good City Council has to be able not only to see the forest for the trees, but also understand that there can be many different types of trees.

Before the gallery, Ellen Remai had been willing to participate in another facet of River Landing. She proposed a spa hotel, but as a new structure. She bought the Legion Hall on Parcel Y, and certainly had the money and business acumen to carry out her proposal. She was willing to do it for her city, even if it wasn't the best of financial moves. We shared the same vision for River Landing as an iconic place in Saskatoon and I was happy when Council approved her proposal in December 2005.

However, as the project dragged on, some

councillors began to openly criticize her. By the time the 2006 civic election rolled around in October, Ellen Remai and the project continued to face relentless headwinds as well as the attitude of some that the city was doing you a favour if they "let" you develop the site. In March 2007, faced with rising costs, Remai Ventures pulled out of the project and the land went back to the city. We were back to square one. But I was not going to give up. Buoyed by my re-election and a fresh new council, I had Chris Dekker, our manager of special projects, put out a call for proposals.

We didn't get a flood of bona fide proposals. Some of them were insulting, treating us as if we were some small town that was willing to make every concession to the developer and give the land to them for free. I had been optimistic that having virtually a zero-vacancy rate for office space in the downtown would have prompted more interest and competition, but that was never the case. No matter how great we think we are, we have to accept the fact that in the minds of many major investors, we're still not Toronto or Vancouver.

I think one of the deterrents for some developers was our insistence on a mixed residential-commercial-retail concept. It would have been much easier to build just a high-rise office tower, but what would that do for rejuvenating our city centre? How would that achieve my goal of 10,000 more permanent residents downtown? I thought of other cities with their concrete towers, and their streets that turn silent and uninviting come the evening.

In September 2007, we finally received a very good proposal. Mike Lobsinger, who had gone to Holy Cross Collegiate in Saskatoon and then went on to become a very successful developer living in Calgary, was willing to take a chance on his old home town and was enthused about coming back to be part of the city's signature development.

I had, and still have, full confidence in Mike. A look at his track record will tell you why. He and his company, Lake Placid Developments, laid out the vision for River Landing that I had hoped for. Anyone who had any money in the stock market in 2008 can tell you what happened next and the market crash affected Lake Placid just like it affected everyone. Investor interest went to zero while bank aversion to projects like River Landing hit an all-time high. Again, it was delay, delay, delay.

It's easy to blame Lobsinger, but it's also unfair. Proposed costs kept mounting. For example, parking was a huge issue. People don't realize that underground parking – which is what Lake Placid had to provide – can cost around $35,000 per stall.

I admit that Mike's feisty character didn't help his cause. He rubbed some of the councillors the wrong way, and to the project's opponents, he epitomized the crass developer who was just in it for the money. I remember one presentation Lake Placid made to City Council. Mike wasn't there; his team recommended he stay back at the hotel and watch it on television.

I never knew we had so many experts on mixed-use

high-rise developments in Saskatoon; even our own city councillors were instant experts! Like a restaurant where because you once ate in one, you think you know how to run one. Private development is a tough business. As for River Landing, everyone had an opinion. It was only Mike, though, who came up with rent projections that, despite the pooh-poohing of some of our "experts," have proven to be bang-on.

Getting the private sector involved was much more arduous than I imagined and, quite frankly, one of my disappointments as mayor. But I don't blame the developers. I have found that different developers have different preferences. Some like to go to the suburbs; others are interested more in city centres. All of them, though, follow the money. Where there's demand, there will be somebody to fill it.

Despite the critics, Mike is a very smart and sensitive business person who knows how to succeed with big projects. When you look at River Landing now, you can, in large measure, thank Mike Lobsinger that the site isn't still a collection of snowdrifts on an empty lot.

Then, Kay Nasser (a very successful businessman and U of S professor Emeritus) came along like a knight in shining armour. When River Landing appeared to have stalled out, Kay first partnered with Mike Lobsinger, and then eventually took the project over on his own. Kay later partnered with others and today we have a tremendous venture we can all be proud of, with a hotel, condos, and office towers.

As the public developments like the water park and promenade progressed, one of my happiest days was driving across the Sid Buckwold Bridge toward downtown, looking at a truly attractive, inviting, and symbolic River Landing. I have no doubt that in the coming decades, everyone will see that we – meaning the citizens of Saskatoon and their elected representatives – did the right thing.

River Landing will be the cornerstone of a sustainable, vibrant downtown – an area of our city that combines residential, office, retail, arts and culture, sports and recreation. That includes Riversdale. I admire civic-minded business leaders like George Marlatte, originally from Saskatoon, who was senior vice-president at the Bank of Nova Scotia at the time. I asked him to keep his branch in Riversdale at a time when the other big banks were abandoning the neighbourhood. He kept the branch open. Another great contributor to Riversdale has been Tom Hutchinson, owner of Magic Lantern Theatres, who took a gamble after talking to me about the future of the neighbourhood and saved the Roxy Theatre from destruction. When I see what's happening in Riversdale today, I get emotional to see the true spirit of Saskatoon – a Saskatoon that shines!

> The downtown should be welcoming to everyone.

The Cineplex development (now known as Scotiabank Theatre) is another example of how development can unfold, despite the naysayers. It was the first brand new theatre built by the corporation anywhere in North America or Europe. At first, it was a tough sell on my part. I lobbied hard with Cineplex executives to convince them to build in the new River Landing. They were of the mind that if they were to build anywhere, it should be the suburbs. I said they needed to look at what was happening at River Landing. Thankfully, they did, and decided to take a gamble. It paid off. Their theatre complex in downtown Saskatoon became one of their most successful properties ever and completely changed their development strategy. It also made me a soothsayer, when you think back to my advice to former Mayor Dayday.

In truth, I have had big ideas for all of downtown Saskatoon. I have been pleased with the great work in rejuvenating our city centre by the work of the Partnership Downtown Business Improvement District (now called DTNYXE). As the City Council representative, I was on the Partnership board along with Terry Scaddan. Executive Director Kent Smith-Windsor and Board Chair Dick Batten put a lot of work into ensuring the provincial government got it right with property reassessment and taxation. Their efforts were instrumental in saving our downtown.

In the future, I hope we will always pursue grand visions, rather than just settling for second best. For example, we could expand what TCU Place (the original Centennial Auditorium) and include a classic gothic-style opera house structure to house larger concerts and conventions. In the space along Idylwyld Drive and the Midtown, I can see a large enclosed city square area that would seamlessly connect the downtown and Riversdale.

If this all seems too far-fetched, remember what one of our greatest mayors, Sid Buckwold, accomplished. I grew up knowing the Buckwold family, and admire what a great city leader we had in Mayor Buckwold. If it weren't for his drive and leadership skills, our downtown today might still be a large railway yard and a downtown where no one would want to work, live, or play. At the opening of the Midtown Plaza in November 1968, he told the crowd, "We were a city divided by the tracks and we needed the tracks removed to create that sense of oneness." I like to think that River Landing has advanced Buckwold's vision and honoured his legacy.

Saskatoon can indeed be a great city, but to do that it has to have a great heart. Our downtown should be everyone's downtown – a place for all residents from all parts of the city. To me, that is the single most important factor in our city's desired future, and it was always the core of my commitment as mayor.

There's a reason why my announcement to run for re-election as Mayor of Saskatoon in 2006 was made at River Landing. It best represented what I stood for as a civic leader, and will always fight for as a proud citizen of Saskatoon.

River Landing Timeline

December 2005: Saskatoon city council approves a plan by Remai Ventures Inc. to build a 200-room hotel and spa complex on Parcel Y. The project is estimated to be 20 stories tall and cost as much as $40 million.

March 2007: Remai Ventures pulls out of the hotel-spa project, citing rising construction costs. The land reverts back to the city.

September 2007: Calgary-based Lake Placid Developments submits a proposal to build a high-rise condo and hotel with a retail component on Parcel Y.

October 2009: Lake Placid misses a deadline to make the final land payment and loses the down payment.

March 2010: Local philanthropist Karim (Kay) Nasser, Owner of Victory Majors Investment Corp., says he wants to revive the project.

April 2010: The value of Parcel Y is reappraised at $11 million, up from $4.8 million.

May 2010: Council agrees to start negotiations

with Lake Placid and Victory Majors, with the land priced at $5.2 million.

November 2010: Victory Majors buys out Lake Placid and saves the project with only minutes to spare before an agreement with the city expires. Nasser estimates the $200-million hotel-office-condo project (the same one first proposed by Lake Placid) will take three years to complete.

April 2015: City council agrees to allow the project to proceed in phases.

January 2016: A partnership with Group Germain Hotels is announced. The hotel chain joins Regina's Greystone Managed Investments, Calgary-based Triovest Realty Advisors, and Victory Majors in the venture. Colliers International will also join the group behind the project. The project is now expected to cost about $300 million.

April 2016: City council votes to grant the developers a tax break estimated at $5.8 million on the office component of the development, similar to other downtown projects. Only Councillor Charlie Clark (running for mayor at the time) votes against the tax break. Only Mayor Don Atchison (also running for mayor as incumbent) and Councillor Tiffany Paulsen, remain on council from the group that approved the original plan in 2005.

June 29, 2016: Groundbreaking ceremony is held.

Source: Phil Tank, *Saskatoon StarPhoenix,* June 29, 2016
http://thestarphoenix.com/news/local-news/
long-delayed-parcel-y-mega-project-just-starting

Working Together

IN THE WEEKS FOLLOWING MY unsuccessful bid for a fifth term, I received several letters thanking me for my years as councillor and especially as mayor. Steve Hogle, then President of the Saskatoon Blades, wrote: *The two of us are very familiar with the wide variety of people who have donned the colours of the Saskatoon Blades over five plus decades. I am hard-pressed to find any alumni who could rival your ability to build teams, gain consensus, and improve community.* If I am fortunate to be remembered in the future for anything as a civic leader, I hope it would be that.

The divisions in our city were many and became more pronounced the longer I served as a councillor. One of my principal reasons for running for mayor was to try to bridge the gaps, heal the wounds, and align everyone with a vision of Saskatoon's potential. In a major campaign speech in 2003, which addressed a number of contentious issues, I stated, "Benefitting one group at the expense of another is not the way to go." I applied this principal to all my considerations as a civic leader. That said, it is inevitable that when there are two sides (and there are always at least two sides), it will always seem like one group won out over the other. I tried to take the long view: what will be best for everyone in our city, not just right now, but years and decades from now?

I also tried to be up-front on all issues, so that everyone was clear as to where I stood. Nevertheless, the *Star Phoenix* would accuse me of being secretive. I was never sure why. I was always glad to conduct interviews with media and would regularly go on talk shows, including a monthly spot on John Gormley's show. I was constantly out in the public, attending hundreds of events. I attended every Council meeting, which were all televised on Shaw Cable 10. How was I not transparent?

I thought of our city's wards as a family. In a good family, everyone should get something, but not always the same thing at the same time. To help build a favourable vote among councillors on the new bridges, for example, I also included sound barriers along the routes and other amenities, so that the benefits of building the new bridges was spread across the city, making it easier for councillors to justify their approval of the new bridges to their constituents. I liked to think it was better to build consensus than strong-arm people as a mayor — to avoid using "the bully pulpit."

I'm a big fan of public-private partnerships because the model shares risks as well as rewards, and quite simply because it's a better way to get things done. Think of how much has been gained by changing the way we traditionally built schools as stand-alone structures with government absorbing the complete cost. Compare that outdated model with T.C. Douglas public high school and Bethlehem Catholic high school, connected by the Shaw Centre, which boasts the finest Olympic swimming pool in North America. Then travel to the east end of Saskatoon to see Centennial Collegiate, connected to the SaskTel Sports Facility, which Soccer Canada couldn't believe we could accomplish in a city of our size.

Building consensus as a family meant getting councillors – and all citizens, really – to understand that improving the quality of life in any ward, especially one that needs it the most, will in fact improve quality of life in all wards. I tried to use language that reinforced the idea of this being one city for all. Rather than referring to Saskatoon's "east side" or "west side," I started referring more to our "east end" and "west end." I particularly disliked the term "inner city" with its negative connotations; it demeans some of our most historical neighbourhoods.

There's no question that Riversdale was hitting an all-time low as a neighbourhood in 2003, plagued with drug and alcohol related crimes, and in need of regeneration. But the sooner we saw Riversdale as part of "our city" rather than "inner city," the sooner we could take the steps we eventually took.

On the first day I became mayor, the other relationships that needed work were with the city's unions, the police service, Métis and First Nations, the University of Saskatchewan, and the federal and provincial governments. As time went on, I discovered countless other partnership opportunities, too.

The Unions

Although it had been nine years since the major strike by civic unions in 1994, the mood at the bargaining table remained distrustful and adversarial, even with the 2000 election of Jim Madden and a council that was largely pro-union.

Labour's tensions were raised considerably with my election as mayor because of my "pro-business" label, which many workers and union leaders translated into "anti-union." Nobody, it seemed, was interested in the truth – that I grew up with a respect for unions. When I was growing up, my father was a union member when he was with the CNR. Yes, I was a businessman, but when you're in small business, you're just as likely to be as wary of major corporations as your union neighbour next door.

The biggest fear among the workers at City Hall

was that I would decimate the workforce and subcontract the work to the private sector. Certainly, when it came to management, I encouraged the use of consultants on a limited, well-defined basis to allow our managers to concentrate on their main responsibilities rather than try to wear different hats; sometimes it's better and less costly to buy experience and expertise than try to develop it yourself. Those managers who saw themselves more as operational than managerial saw this approach as a threat, but over time they generally came around to my point of view. As far as being anti-union in order to promote a private sector agenda was concerned, though, that was never my intent.

I made it a priority to attend union events, sometimes much to their surprise, whenever invited. More than once I was told, "Gee, we never expected to see you here!" to which I would respond, "Of course I'm here. You invited me!" I also tried to visit as many city employees in as many locations as I could during the Christmas season. On my first visit to one City department, I overheard an employee say to her colleague, "Well, that's the one and only time we'll ever see him in here!" The following year, I heard her colleague say, "I thought you said we'd never see him again."

My position with the unions was that I was going to be open and frank. I would say, "Why don't we start with the truth? That just makes everything easier." My position was clear: I was not opposed to unions, and not opposed to wage increases. I understand very well what it's like to try

to pay a mortgage, make car payments, and raise a family.
Who doesn't feel they deserve more? And often they do!
However, as mayor I also had the responsibility of acting in
the best interests of all citizens of Saskatoon, in all sectors.
Our mutual goal, then, was to find the best possible middle
ground. The most effective union leaders that I dealt with
understood the importance of reaching the point of mutual
benefit, and did an excellent job of representing their
constituents, just as I tried to do with mine.

The best example was the very serious issue of
pensions, which when I first became mayor had the
potential to seriously impact Saskatoon's future ability to
invest in our infrastructure and other development. The
issue centered around targeted benefits versus defined
benefits. There are countless other cities that are now in
serious financial difficulty because they still cannot reach
agreement with their unions on this matter.

In simple terms, a defined benefit pension plan
means that when you retire you get a pre-determined
amount of money, based upon your years of experience
and previous earnings. The marketplace could sustain these
plans when the people in the workforce were younger and
when people didn't live as long. That has all changed, and
will become even more of an issue as the remaining Baby
Boomers retire and will be living longer on their pensions.
In today's world, organizations cannot realistically maintain
a pension plan that commits our future leaders to pre-
determined financial commitments.

The only viable alternative is what the industry calls a targeted benefit program. That's where the employee and employer negotiate to both pay into an investment plan to fund the employee's retirement. How much the employee receives in retirement depends on the performance of those investments, in the hope, but not the guarantee, that the targeted amount will be achieved.

A lot of hard work on both sides went into reaching agreement between the City and our police and fire protective services to make the move from a defined benefit to a targeted benefit plan, but we did.

It's a personal point of pride for me that I was given a CUPE windbreaker at their 2015 Christmas party at the Nicholson Yards, symbolizing for me how I was able to improve relationships with the unions during my four terms. I had been talking to them earlier in the year about my attitudes towards unions and their importance. They asked me, "If we gave you one of our CUPE jackets, would you wear it?" I told them that of course I would. Why wouldn't I?

My harshest critics weren't the unions. It was the business sector, or what my largely left-leaning detractors liked to call my "big business buddies." The media and the general public always had trouble pigeon-holing me, because I never identified with any political party and because the way I voted had nothing to do with "left" or "right" but rather what I felt was best for the city.

Even so, there are those who want to live in a simple

world of black and white, and are desperate to put you into a neat box that they can criticize. To some of my business colleagues, then, I would be "acting like a socialist" and at other times it would be the NDP crowd who saw me as being in the pocket of the corporate movers and shakers. Just as Ricky Nelson sang in *Garden Party*, "You can't please everyone, so you got to please yourself."

First Nations and Métis

Within weeks of becoming mayor in the fall of 2003, the provincial government launched a Commission of Inquiry, led by Justice David Wright, into the November 1990 freezing death of 17-year-old Neil Stonechild. After several months, the inquiry concluded that there was not enough evidence to charge the police officers involved with any wrongdoing. In effect, there was no closure for anyone on either side of the issue, and feelings continued to run high.

Compounding these feelings was the highly controversial casino issue, and whether or not the Indigenous people could build a casino downtown. The fierce debate in Council and in the community evoked cries of racism.

Nobody can or should deny that there was a gap between the non-Indigenous people of Saskatoon and the Métis and First Nations. That gap was widening, as the population of Indigenous peoples in our city was rising, from just under 12,000 in 1991 to over 20,000 in 2003. It was going to take considerable work, on all sides, to avoid serious conflicts.

I knew, too, that it wasn't just a matter of respect for one another. Words can do only so much. It was also about the hard, tangible things like a good job that puts food on the table for your family, and a home that keeps them warm and safe at night – the things that matter to everyone, every day.

Chief Szabo is to be commended for his sincere effort during those tense times to mend fences between the Saskatoon Police and the Indigenous community. When he finished his term as Chief of Police, he was given a star blanket to show the Indigenous community's appreciation. It was well-deserved.

One of my first steps in the healing process was to request a visit to the police station just before Christmas 2003. Chief Szabo said he would be out of town, but that I was welcome to come. I was greeted by Deputy Police Chief Gary Broste. Gary and I had known each other since we were kids; his father was my first hockey coach. That helped to get things off to a good start. I talked to a number of the officers, to get their feelings, and to tell them that things would get better and we would move forward.

I have the greatest respect for police officers. While everyone else would immediately run away from the sound of a gunshot, we expect the police to run toward it. Our police, in turn, deserve as much protection from their bosses – that is, City Hall and City Council and the Board of Police Commissioners – as we can give them. I always supported the Saskatoon Police Service's recommendations for any advanced equipment and vehicles to make their job safer, and to ensure accountability. That's consistent with the wishes of our citizens, who in poll after poll, place public safety and policing among their top priorities.

My next step was to approach the First Nations and Métis in our community, and in particular the Federation of Sovereign Indigenous Nations (FSIN). We in Saskatoon have been very fortunate to have outstanding leadership in local chiefs Leduc, Lafonde, Kapesewin, and Bear.

Before my time as mayor, I had not had a lot of interaction with the Indigenous community. As a kid, I had an older cousin who married a First Nations fellow who started out as a labourer and went on to own his own business. I would hang out with them sometimes; they always made me feel so welcome. I was fortunate, too, to grow up in a home where we respected others regardless of their race or creed.

My first opportunity to do business with First Nations other than, of course, the customers who came to our store, was as the councillor for Ward 10. I was asked – told, actually – by the City to contact Chief Lafonde of the Muskeg Reserve in Sutherland regarding a long overdue payment owed to the city. Apparently, the Muskeg Reserve had not paid for its portion of the cost to build the overpass at McKercher Drive and College Drive. I was taken aback by the assignment. "I know I'm the councillor for Ward 10, but what am I, a bill collector too?" I guess I was.

When I met with Councillor Mark Arcand from the Saskatoon Tribal Council, I explained the situation. Here's the thing: there was nothing in writing. He replied, "Well, if you say we owe the money, I guess we do." There was no asking for proof of liability, no dickering, no indignation. Councillor Arcand simply took me at my word. It was all done on a handshake. He asked if it could be paid over time, which I said would be possible. I will never forget this experience; it set the tone for my involvement as mayor with our First Nations from then on. Be direct. Be honest. Never betray the trust.

From the inception of the urban reserve in Saskatoon, city councillors and councillors from the Muskeg Band council would get together each year for a Christmas luncheon. We made a point of sitting alternately, to better get to know each other and exchange ideas. It's far better, I have found, to build relationships around a meal or some social setting, rather than in an office, where there's a desk between you – sort of like, as kids, the difference between being in the playground or being in the principal's office. You don't always have to have an agenda, either. Sometimes, I would get together with the chiefs just to talk about family, about sports, whatever came to mind at the moment. I remember some evening dinners where we were also accompanied by our wives.

Chief Leduc, Chief Kapesewin, and I would go

golfing at least once a year at Dakota Dunes. One time, I asked Chief Kapesewin if everything was going well, to which the Chief brought up the problem he was having with a property the Band had bought at Avenue W and 22nd Street. They wanted it be designated as an urban reserve. I said, "Really? Well why don't you make a few phone calls to set something up and we'll fly down to Ottawa with you to get things moving?"

A couple of months went by and I hadn't heard anything more about it, so I phoned someone in administration at Muskeg. He phoned back soon after to say, "We didn't think you were really serious about it, so we haven't done anything." I told him I wouldn't have asked if I wasn't serious. Shortly after that call, George Lafonde set up a meeting with INAC (Indian and Aboriginal Affairs Canada).

We flew to Ottawa and met with INAC where Lafonde presented his case. I added, "I just want to expedite this, so I can tell you that at our end it will take me about 30 seconds at Saskatoon City Council to read the hearing into the books, and it won't take us much longer than that to approve it — because I don't think anyone's going to come forward to complain. So why don't you pick up the pace at your end and we'll get this all wrapped up?"

The INAC staff asked for a few minutes by themselves, and huddled in the corner. They came back to the table to say, "We don't believe we've ever heard this before. It's very unusual." The application was approved.

When it came to the regular meeting of Saskatoon City Council, I called three times for anyone to come forward to address council on the issue. Nobody did. The motion was called for, seconded, and passed.

Saskatoon should be proud of its record regarding urban reserves. A number of mayors and councillors from other cities have contacted us about the structure of an urban reserve and its value. I always encouraged them to embrace the idea. The most important reason, I would tell them, is "Urban reserves create jobs, and the more people who are working in our city, the more we are all the same."

That doesn't mean I supported every initiative from the tribal councils. I have never, and will never, support the idea of a casino in downtown Saskatoon and I remain opposed to casinos in principle. The casino location was finally decided: Whitecap Reserve 26 kms south of Saskatoon.

Regardless of your opinion of casinos in general, the casino on Whitecap Reserve has produced great benefits for First Nations and the Whitecap community in particular. I have sometimes joked that after all the debates in council and in the media, we came up with the true Canadian solution: no one was entirely happy with it, but everyone could live with it. I also don't think that it hurt my relationships with First Nations leaders, either and I was delighted to be included in the grand opening of the casino.

So often, politicians have said they will do

something positive for Indigenous Peoples, but what has really been done, or done well? St. Mary's Elementary School is an example of a putting your money where your mouth is. Situated in the heart of Riversdale, St. Mary's had the highest percentage of First Nations and Métis students in the city. Built in 1913, it had also seen much better days and needed renovation and repair. Rather than just patching it up, we asked, "Why can't we give these kids a new school they could really be proud of – a school just as fine as any other in Saskatoon?"

With the help of the provincial and federal governments, the Greater Saskatoon Catholic School Board found the $19 million to build the St. Mary's Wellness and Education Centre, which officially opened in December 2012 and is a cornerstone for the rejuvenation of the entire community.

I am so proud to be a citizen of a city that can achieve visions like St. Mary's. Thanks to the work of so many teachers, administrators, politicians, planners, and volunteers, the new St. Mary's facility will, I know, pay us back in countless ways, for decades to come. If you don't believe me, you need to be there during a regular school day to see, as I have seen, the pride that over 350 children and their teachers now take in their new home.

Do we still have a long way to go to achieve a fully integrated community? Yes. It is indeed a long — perhaps endless — path, but we can always continue to take steps, and take them together. We made progress in attracting

First Nations officers to our police service. We also hired our first Indigenous firefighter. I hope that in the future we will have at least proportional First Nations representation on City Council. To my knowledge, Moe Neault has been the only councillor who self-declared as Métis.

I also hope to see representation from other peoples in our multicultural city. For example, it would be great to see a Filipino councillor, someone from Syria on our school board – you get the idea.

University of Saskatchewan

I am grateful to Premier Walter Scott and all those involved in the decision in 1905 to establish the University of Saskatchewan in Saskatoon.

I hasten to acknowledge the contribution of our other post-secondary institutions, notably Saskatchewan Polytechnic, the Saskatchewan Indian Institute of Technology, and Gabriel Dumont Institute. It is the University of Saskatchewan, though, that has influenced our city from the very beginning, attracting the best and brightest minds from throughout our province and the world, and giving us a world view along with global connections through its faculty and alumni. It has also been one of our largest employers for more than century. Each fall, it brings about 22,000 students to its campus, to our city – yet another reason why the U of S is such a major contributor to our economy.

Just as I made a point of going out to visit our other major employers such as PotashCorp (now Nutrien) and Cameco, I wanted to build a better "town and gown" relationship with the U of S. Many saw the university and its campus as separate from, rather than part of, Saskatoon. That doesn't make sense.

I looked for opportunities to make connections. I remember attending an announcement on campus, at which various dignitaries spoke. Immediately after, then-president Peter McKinnon came up to me, apologizing for not including me in the program. "I didn't come here to speak," I said. "I just wanted to show support as the mayor for what you're doing." Peter assured me that, "Any time you want to speak at any of our events from here on, you will be most welcome to do so!"

Great things happen when you choose the right partners. There is no better example of this collaboration that the Canadian Light Source (the only synchrotron in Canada and one of the largest infrastructure investments in our country's history). These great accomplishments often have their beginnings in a casual conversation, and I wanted to ensure that we could have those conversations regularly. My goal was to meet with the President of the University of Saskatchewan at least once a month. I thought it especially important to meet with Ilene Busch Vishniak when she became president, because she was new not only to the University, but also to the city. We would get together monthly, usually on a Thursday or Friday, for breakfast. That way, we got to know each other's priorities and identify ways the City and the university could support each other.

We would talk about infrastructure and major projects like Preston Crossing – the size of the stores, hotels, and impact on the city and university. Phil Richards, our city manager, and I had a memorable meeting with U of S President Peter McKinnon and Richard Florizon, the university's vice president of finance and resources (who went on to become the President of Dalhousie University). I desperately wanted to see top-quality new housing for students near the campus. Florizon replied that the U of S couldn't afford it, that the numbers didn't work. I said, "What if we wrote you a cheque for a million dollars? Would the numbers work then?" That's how we got College Quarter Residence built — in a conversation over breakfast. Of course, there were other key players as well, most significantly the provincial government and Minister Don Morgan.

Those casual conversations also helped to sort out transit issues and create the bus mall on campus, a new fire hall, and funding for other programs like VIDO and Intervac (Vaccine and Infectious Disease Organization-International Vaccine Centre).

People might ask me, "Which university president did you like the best?" and I will always reply that it doesn't matter. Personalities should not get in the way of developing big-picture strategic relationships. As far as I was concerned, this was not about Don meeting with Peter or Ilene or whomever, but about the city meeting with the university.

I hope that Saskatoon continues to build on its national reputation for creating great relationships. Smart leaders understand that cities and universities can't do much on their own. We all have to work together, involving all levels of government. Do that, and you will wake up one day, realizing that out of Canada's ten biggest science and technology projects, two of them are in Saskatoon.

Federal and Provincial Governments

It's too bad that personalities can get in the way of forming effective inter-governmental relationships, but it has certainly happened in the past, especially when you get a mayor who is aligned with a particular political party. I counted it as one of my strengths that nobody could say I openly supported any political party, although there were those who liked to put a label on me. During my 13 years as mayor, I was asked by each of the major political parties at different times to be their candidate, but that did not interest me at all.

I did not publicly support any political party, but I did support every government, provincial or federal. There's a very big difference. I remember being in the Toronto Pearson Airport, waiting to fly back to Saskatoon, when this MP from another province approached me and blurted, "I've got you mayors figured out. You're whores! You sell yourself to the highest bidder!" To that I said, "You're absolutely right. How much do you have to give me?"

If you want the money, you have to play the game, and bad-mouthing or blaming the federal or provincial government is just plain bad practice for any mayor or city council. I tried to be as honest and open as I could when I talked with other levels of government. In turn, I took them at their word. If they said there was nothing left in the cookie jar, then that's the way it was. No sense in whining. On the other hand, I went out of my way to express thanks when the city was the beneficiary of the government. I always treated the annual grants as a gift, not an entitlement. If you were to look at my State of the City addresses, you would see that I consistently acknowledged the assistance from the federal and provincial governments.

For years, setting the city budget early enough to do effective planning was very difficult because you never knew what the provincial government's budget was going to be. As a councillor and mayor, I worked with 22 provincial budgets.

The provincial finance minister does not deliver the budget until the end of March. For decades, that meant the cities could not confidently do their planning until April, when a quarter of the year had already gone by. I give credit to then Premier Brad Wall, because he listened to the municipal governments in Saskatchewan, and in his second term brought about a consistent revenue sharing formula so that we could confidently do our budgets in November and December prior to our new fiscal year.

In almost every case, I was the one who had to take the initiative to develop good relationships with whatever party was in power. Sometimes, I had to be pushy. When I became mayor, I tried several times to contact Premier Lorne Calvert. He just wasn't returning my calls, so I phoned one of the Saskatoon NDP MLAs, Judy Junor, and told her about my frustration. "Judy, please relay to the premier that if he doesn't want to talk to me over the phone, I guess we'll just have to talk to each other through the mass media."

After that, I got the hoped-for call from Premier Calvert. He claimed that before I talked to Judy Junor, he had not been getting my phone messages. He and I developed an excellent relationship. Mardele has had Lorne's wife, Betty, to our home for coffee. I flew with him on the government plane to support the province's major announcement in Lloydminster and Fort McMurray in 2007 regarding the connector highway from La Loche to Fort McMurray.

Whether it was the federal or provincial government, I never publicly criticized their budgets. They're under constant pressure to help everyone. Sure, it's easy to be an armchair quarterback, but why would I want to bash them? It might be great for a mayor to make himself or herself look good to their constituents, but it's bad for their city.

Complaining gets you nowhere, except out the door. I made it a point to take my time before I made public comments about a budget, rather than give a knee-jerk reaction. Even when I felt like making a call to any government minister or leader, I would say to myself, "Maybe I should bite my tongue, be a leader, and do what's best."

Local news reporter Cam Hutchison put it very well: "During Atchison's time as mayor, almost $1 billion in federal and provincial cash came Saskatoon's way. Why pick a fight?"

Just as with the provincial government at first, I was not shy about making myself – and Saskatoon – known within the upper circles of the federal government, including the Prime Minister's Office. Early in my first term, Toronto Mayor David Miller, who was also first elected in 2003, convened a meeting of big city mayors with Paul Martin, who had become prime minister in December of 2003. Saskatoon, however, was not invited; we still weren't considered "big city." Regardless, I wanted to meet our new prime minister.

My chance came when I heard that Prime Minister Martin was attending an event in Prince Albert in January 2004. I called prominent local Liberal lawyer and lobbyist Doug Richardson, and arranged for the two of us to drive to Prince Albert so Doug could introduce me. No one in Saskatoon was better connected to people in power than Doug Richardson; his efforts, usually behind the scenes, worked magic in our city and this was just one example.

Prime Minister Martin was impressed with the fact that I would go to that much trouble just to say hello, and our relationship grew from there.

On another occasion, during a developing blizzard, I flew to Regina and back just to say hello to the federal minister in charge of housing. I asked Paul Gauthier, the city's general manager of community services, to come with me because I wanted to explain what we would like to do with attainable housing. We saw our plan for Saskatoon as being on the leading edge in Canada. (In fact, it became the best affordable housing program in the country.) It never hurt to meet ministers of the federal government and to tell them about Saskatoon.

At the start of that day, the executive assistant in the Mayor's Office, Carol, had received a call from Ottawa to say the federal minister was going to be in Regina and could I come down to see him. Timing would be difficult on our end: I was to open the Western Retail Lumber Association (WRLA) the next morning by sawing a two-by-four (not a ribbon, it's a lumber show!) so I needed to be back in Saskatoon that night. Added to that scheduling pressure, there was a big blizzard coming and 40 below weather. On top of that, there were no scheduled evening flights to take us back home from Regina.

I didn't want to disappoint the minister or the WRLA, so Paul and I decided that we would fly down and take a rental car back late at night. We arrived at the hanger of our local aviation company, West Wind, and we were waiting to board the flight when Dennis Goll, West Wind's founder and CEO, came in and thanked us for flying with his airline. I mentioned we would be driving back later that night because there was no return flight. Dennis came back a few minutes later and said that he had a plane in Yorkton that was going to be coming to Saskatoon, but he would divert it to Regina to pick us up. What a gracious offer!

In Regina, the meeting with the minister went long. When Paul and I arrived at the Regina airport, there was no airplane in sight. We went into the West Wind office to see if they were even open. Fortunately, they had wondered what happened but hadn't given up on us. In fact, they had pulled the plane into the hanger to keep it warm. What service! We boarded and took off for Saskatoon. The pilot pointed out that there was a full bar on board and we were more than welcome to drink whatever we would like. I don't drink but, after such a grueling day, I suggested to Paul that he should test the red wine just to make sure that it was okay for the next passengers. We had to detour around the storm and arrived into Saskatoon very late. A few hours later, I was sawing a two-by-four.

It's not surprising politicians interpreted my support for the party in power as support for that party generally. That's their nature. After Prime Minister Harper and the Conservatives took over from the Liberals, I attended a reception for Agricultural Minister Gerry Ritz at Prairieland Park. The Conservatives had noticed how I had always been nice to the previous government and obviously concluded I must be a devout Liberal. From what I could tell at that reception, they really didn't want to have much to do with me. It's like, "If you thanked those people all the time, you must be one of them, or else you wouldn't be so grateful and kind to them."

I made a point of seeking out the Minister's assistant. "I want you to know," I said to her, "the more successful Minister Ritz is, the more successful I can be, and I'll do whatever we can to make sure he succeeds here in Saskatoon." She started walking away, then stopped, turned, and said, "Give me your card. I've got to get to know you better." She eventually ended up in the Prime Minister's Office.

In a system where government-bashing is a national sport, it is not surprising that it was hard for any federal or provincial government to understand that I sincerely wanted to support them and help them succeed, regardless of their political stripe. The politicians were not used to this at all. They were used to every mayor picking on the federal or provincial government – and never offering any solutions, just crying repeatedly for more money. Conversely, my approach was, "What do I need to do in order to get to where I need to be?" along with "What do we need to do to get us where you need to be?"

Compassion shows a road that leads to success, it is a hand up not a hand out.

When it looked like Harper's government was not going to come through with the needed funds for the proposed

Mendel Art Gallery renovation, I flew to Ottawa in 2007 to meet with Bev Oda, Minister of Canadian Heritage and said, "You need to explain to me why you made me spend a million dollars on drawings for renovations when you're not even interested in giving us the money." She excused herself for a moment and huddled with her deputy minister. A few minutes later she came back and replied, "You didn't need to do all of that. A stick drawing would have been sufficient." I told her that is not what we were told.

Later that year, Minister Oda attended the announcement for the new Persephone Theatre. That seemed to help push things in our favour. Eventually, funding came through for the new Remai Modern Art Gallery, with the help of the Honourable Carol Skelton and MP Lyn Yellich.

> We need to trade in knives and guns for hammers and saws, and get youth to work

Another memorable time was the day I got a phone call from a high-ranking federal official to say we were not going to get the funding we needed to build the new south bridge (Gordie Howe Bridge). I immediately got on the phone to Carol Skelton (MP for Rosetown-Biggar from 2000 to 2008 and Minister of Western Economic Diversification at the time (2006). When I spoke to Minister Skelton, I asked her, "Which mayor never complains about the federal government and only thanks them for what they do for Saskatoon and which mayor only complains about the federal government?" The Minister and I had met many times and I always made a point of talking to her about building a new bridge. She could appreciate the advantages as someone from a rural community who often came into Saskatoon and regarded it as "her city." I knew she shared my conviction that federal support for a new bridge was justified and deserved. All it took to move this project forward was that one phone call from me to her office, and federal funding for the Gordie Howe Bridge was back on the table – and was approved.

I found myself flying to Ottawa frequently in order to support funding requests for Saskatoon. If you're from the prairies and the person you're speaking with is not, you sometimes have to remind them that Canada's western border is not at the end of a runway at Pearson International.

International

The rise in Saskatoon's prominence on the global stage gave me the opportunity to make lasting friends with a number of consulate representatives and every time visiting dignitaries came to our city, I would make an effort to meet them.

Once I golfed with members of the Chinese consulate. It was in the afternoon, and I had broken my toe in the morning, but that didn't deter me. I was the first person the Chinese Consul General met in western Canada when he first visited Saskatoon. I was always flattered by how well I was treated because of my relationship with

Pacific Rim representatives; whenever my travels took me via China they would assist me through Chinese customs.

I also golfed with Taiwanese trade mission representative, Jeffrey Kau. We became good friends, and would try to arrange a golf date at least once a year.

Saskatoon's increased profile internationally meant that, as mayor, I had to play a bigger role than any of my predecessors in promoting our city abroad. I was called by Ted Neiman from Canpotex, asking if I would have supper with Mr. Kwok (who at that time was the single largest purchaser of potash in the world, importing five to eight million tonnes a year, and Canpotex's number one customer), in an effort to speed up contract negotiations. I said, "No problem, name the day." When he said, "July 4th," I asked if he could make the dinner reservation for July 3rd or July 5th, or if July 4th was the only dinner option to make it a luncheon. July 4th is Mardele's and my anniversary and that is the only celebration I have never missed; I have missed birthdays and other special events, but I've never missed our wedding anniversary. Thankfully, we agreed to lunch at the Saskatoon Club on July 4th.

What would you say to someone like Mr. Kwok, when he looks at you and asks, "If I sign this deal, will you promise to have lunch with me in Singapore?"

I said, "Absolutely! I would be thrilled!" Mr. Kwok signed the contract and I began to organize my visit to Singapore for our dinner. Luckily, I had been asked, as Mayor of Saskatoon, to visit investors and officials in Taiwan and the Philippines and could add Singapore to the itinerary. The following year, Mr. Kwok and I encountered each other at the Olympic Games in Vancouver and sat together for lunch. Our meeting laid the foundation for a lifelong, business relationship. (On this trip, as other trips abroad, I never had an entourage. I would go alone. Sometimes I worked with SREDA and Tourism Saskatoon, but not often.) On this trip, my first to Asia, I took Councillor Myles Heidt with me. Myles was a great councillor who was direct and straightforward — he told you exactly how he saw an issue.

It's been said that when you look out your front window in Saskatoon, you can see forever. It is very important that we continue to look far beyond our city limits. To be truly an international city some day, we have to begin to understand how the global economy works, and how we can best fit into it. To this day, I treasure the small but meaningful "gifts of good luck" (such as small paper calendars and pens) I received from Asian dignitaries, expressing their desire to continue good relationships with our city. I hope these relationships do indeed continue.

I am big on protocol but even I have learned a few new things. I was appalled to learn that Canadian mayors, in general, had a bad reputation with Queen Elizabeth. Often due to inappropriate hugging and being over familiar. To be honest, I just about did hug Her Majesty once, though it would have been totally unintentional. She was getting off the plane in Saskatoon during the Royal Visit to Saskatchewan in 2005. The wind was so strong it blew Mardele's hat off. A sudden gust caused the plane's stairs to lurch, and the Queen just about lost her balance. I lunged forward to catch her, but fortunately she was able to grab the stair railing and steady herself. Otherwise, I think I would have made the front page of every newspaper in the UK, with a picture of the Queen in my arms and a headline reading "Queen Falls For Mayor!" As a goaltender, it would have been my biggest save.

Police and Communities

No community wants to be crowned the "Crime Capital of Canada" — but before, during and now after my time as mayor, Saskatoon has remained among the leaders in per-capita criminal offenses. Yes, I can say that the crime level actually dropped after I became mayor, and I was surprised when we dropped to number two. But even one crime is one too many if you're the victim, and no neighbourhood deserves to live in fear.

In coming to Saskatoon's defense, I have justifiably noted several facts that need to be considered. First of all, our community has always been one that has been encouraged to report any incident, large or small. In major cities, I argue, most people don't even bother reporting a broken window, a loud party next door, or a stolen bicycle, because they think it's just a waste of time. One city that I won't mention didn't even include gang-related crime in their statistics! Why should they get a pass in the crime ratings, and not us? Secondly, it's primarily younger adults (and within that group, primarily males) who commit the most crimes, and Saskatoon has had the youngest population of any city in Canada. On top of that, we have had young people, primarily males, who were earning exceptional money in the oilfields, resulting in rapidly rising cases of drug abuse.

Illegal use of drugs, by far, is principal driver of criminal activity. When the downturn in the oilfields led to layoffs, those who were already addicted no longer had a job, but they still had the addiction. They returned to cities like Saskatoon, where the gangs were more than happy to serve them.

Also, in comparison to a metropolis like Toronto, we're a small city where a "crime wave" can be caused by just a small group of perpetrators. I remember an alarming rash of vehicle break-ins that occurred over a few months – all caused by just three youths.

Finally – and I know this is of no comfort to those who have been victimized by crime – most crimes in Saskatoon have tended to be confined to specific neighbourhoods, and where the victims already knew and had relationships with the perpetrators. In most neighbourhoods in Saskatoon, people go to bed feeling safe. In places like our downtown at certain times, though, the uneasiness for some was and is significant.

I never waivered in my advocacy for a well-equipped, adequately staffed police service. I believe the anecdotal information that states that as the number of officers per 100,000 population goes down, the crime rate goes up.

I also believe that good policing is as much public relations as it is enforcement. I put forward the idea of horse patrols, not so much to fight crime, but to attract young kids, especially those at risk, to develop positive rapport with police officers. That's why I also supported more foot patrols, so that people – be they store-owners, home-owners or anyone in a neighbourhood – would get to know the police as people like them, who were on their side. I would love to see us hire retired police officers in uniform to visit schools.

Establishing our air patrol has been a major advancement in our policing, resulting in fewer high-speed car chases and faster apprehensions through devices such as heat imaging. The career criminals in Saskatoon took notice as well. They would drive by the airport to see if the plane was there or not in order to decide when to commit a robbery or some other crime. That's when we decided to keep the plane out of sight in the hanger.

Let's not deceive ourselves, though. The only way to really combat crime is to combat social injustice and inequality in all its forms. That's why, to me, creating better housing and more jobs has been a priority. People who own their homes tend to stay longer in those homes, and to look after them better. That means their children stay in the same schools longer, create better and more permanent friendships, and have a stronger bond with those who can positively mentor them. Reducing crime is much less about airplanes and advanced technology, and much more about jobs and good homes.

New and Diverse Canadians

The faces and fabric of Saskatoon continue to change. I remember talking to NDP MLA Pat Atkinson, who became Minister of Immigration the same year I was first elected mayor. I recommended to her that she focus on attracting Filipinos to Canada, and to her credit she did. That eventually resulted in many more people from the Philippines coming to Saskatoon.

Conflicts throughout the world have been a major reason why people have emigrated to our province and city, starting with religious persecutions as far back as the late 19th century through to the 20th century events of the Russian Revolution, the two great wars, the Vietnam War, the Serbo-Bosnian conflict, the horrendous events in Africa — the list goes on. Make no mistake. Whenever we have welcomed these people as our new neighbours and co-workers, they have enriched our community through their entrepreneurship, their leadership, and a pioneer spirit that underpins our wonderful prairie city.

I know I have said it countless times throughout this book, but I will unashamedly say it again. We must always look at the big picture. When we do, it is much easier to see how all of us can fit in, and the potential that we have. Our diversity is not only people from overseas, but also our Indigenous Peoples, those who come here from other parts of Canada, and those who come from our rural and northern communities. Just as importantly, we need to remember that people do not emigrate to countries; they emigrate to neighbourhoods.

Acceptance of diversity includes acceptance of each person's sexual identity and lifestyle. I know I was criticized during my term for never being part of the Saskatoon Pride Festival, particularly the Parade. Often, it was because I was already committed to other events. Regardless, I have never uttered a disparaging remark about the Parade or the fine people of our city who support and participate in it.

To me it is obvious that wherever our citizens come from, or whatever their orientation, it is our duty as Canadians to accept them, but also for them to accept us. Tolerance and a willingness to understand and respect those things that are new is a two-way street. We must all work hard at having one community spirit, while enjoying and celebrating our unique cultures, beliefs and aspirations. I am not a Pollyanna. We will never live in some kind of Utopia. But we must never stop trying to get there.

All Good Things

THE PROVERB, "ALL GOOD THINGS MUST come to an end" reminds us to be prepared, because no matter how good life can be, it is always changing.

I spent each of my terms as mayor working as hard as I could to get things done, because I was never certain that I would get another four years in service to my city. Fortunately for me, the electorate saw fit to keep me in office for four terms. Going into the 2016 civic election, I wondered, could there be an unprecedented fifth? The fact is, for almost any politician who has enjoyed a long career, you hear the ever-louder comment, "Maybe it's time for a change." I heard it loud and clear in 2016, but I gave my campaign everything I could muster. I argued that it's a myth to think that change in itself is good, especially if you can be far from certain what that change might be. You have to ask, "Change to what?"

Various writers in the media picked up on the change theme, citing their reasons. I remember one writer in particular saying that I had changed – that in 2016, I was not the same mayor I was when I was first elected in 2003.

"Don Atchison needs his pink slip" was the headline of an article by Devon Stone a month before the Saskatoon Civic Election in October 2016. He began by giving me credit for my role in creating "Saskatchewan's main economic hub." He then went on to write, "Unfortunately, the lag and complacency that usually come with long-term incumbency have started to catch him. This inevitable incumbent's lag catches everyone who serves in public office for too long and Don Atchison is no exception. With the lag comes a clouded view of reality."

I wonder who in fact had a "clouded view of reality." In my 13 years as mayor, and before that for nine years as a councillor, my goals and vision for Saskatoon never changed. What did change, though, was my understanding of how civic politics worked, of how it fit in with the province, the country, and the world.

One criticism was that I had run up the city's debt. It's true, but for that I certainly do not apologize – any more than you would apologize to your family for securing a mortgage for a brand new home because interest rates were low, you had the highest possible credit rating so lenders were very willing to negotiate good terms, and you were secure in your projected income. If that wasn't enough, what if the federal and provincial governments both said they would pay a good portion of the construction costs?

The pages of this book could be filled with examples of lost opportunities for our city because of "frugal leaders." Their inaction, or fear of public backlash, often ended up costing us more in the long run. When I first took office, I could see that safety and security in Saskatoon had been badly neglected; our police service was understaffed and morale was low; the wages to our firefighters were out of step with other cities. Crime had escalated to the point where we had the highest crime rate out of 22 cities in Canada. It began to drop only after I was able to convince City Council to increase the size of the police service and equip them with better tools to do their job.

Experience never grows old

To use my house analogy again, when is the best time to fix your roof? As soon as you spot a leak? Or years later when the real damage has been done? I completely agree that civic governments have to be fiscally responsible, but sometimes being responsible means wisely investing your money, not hoarding it.

You don't collect taxes to put it all in the bank. You use your constituents' hard-earned money to make their community the best possible place to work, live, play, and do business. During my term, that meant investing in the Circle Drive South Bridge (now the Gordie Howe Bridge), the Traffic Bridge, the North Commuter Parkway Bridge (now the Chief Mistawasis Bridge), River Landing, the Farmers' Market, the 25th Street Extension, the new vision for Gordie Howe Bowl, the Shaw Centre, the SaskTel Soccer Facility, the Remai Modern Art Gallery, several new overpasses, 15 new schools including eight with community centres, new police headquarters, affordable/ attainable housing for the residents of Saskatoon and U of S students, and the list goes on.

During all of this, and in fact because of our wise investing in infrastructure, we maintained our triple-A credit rating. Yet people like Mr. Stone would say (and did), "As the city's growth slows and its taxes rise, Saskatoon won't have a future as bright as it did in 2003 when Atchison was first elected."

The future is every bit as bright, if not brighter. Those who read these words many years from now can judge for themselves how our city continues to fulfill its destiny, through the inevitable ups and downs of our economy and other issues.

I wanted it all to keep going, and to play my role in leading the way in my capacity as the mayor. My dreams were as big as ever, and so was my enthusiasm. No such luck. On October 26, 2016 about 3,000 more voters than my supporters went with the winds of change. Charlie Clark, a well-respected city councillor, was chosen to be the next mayor.

I remember driving home with Mardele that night

after conceding the race. It felt surreal to know City Hall was no longer going to be the major part of my life, as it had been for some 22 years since I first sat in the Council chambers. But I also knew that, just as there was life after hockey a long time ago, there would be life after serving as mayor. New doors would open to me, or better yet, I would open them myself. I'm pretty sure Mardele was thinking, "What am I going to do with him if he's going to be around the house all the time?"

I went back to work the next morning because I was officially still mayor; I carried out my remaining days on the job as I had always done. Just before walking out of the Mayor's Office office for the last time, I sent one final message as mayor:

To: Employees of the City of Saskatoon

Thank you for the past 13 years. Since 2003, we have accomplished much together. There is still more work to do as we build a great world city.

Remember the journey is not a sprint, but rather a marathon. I have often said, "Government may move slowly, but we always move forward."

Unfortunately, I couldn't get to see each of you to say

goodbye. I want you to succeed. I want our great city to succeed. I love this city.

Thank you for your contribution and your hard work. Every day your efforts help to improve the lives of the citizens of Saskatoon.

I wish you well. I am now signing off as mayor.

Donald J. Atchison

To Our Future Leaders

ON AUGUST 16TH, 2024, I ONCE MORE put my name on the ballot. I had 22 years of service under my belt, nine as a city councillor and 13 as mayor. I had the honour of being the longest serving Mayor of the City of Saskatoon.

So why did I run?

While there were certainly outside influences, the current state of the city was largely a reflection of a series of poor decisions by City Council. But I felt it wasn't too late to alter our course; we had a chance to make Saskatoon safe, clean, and affordable and I wanted to lead that change. I felt this election wasn't just about the next four years; it was about the next 40 and beyond. I had driven positive change before, and I was committed to doing so again.

In the end, the citizens chose a different candidate for mayor, but I have no regrets for putting in the effort. Through media appearances, debates, and conversations, I brought forth the issues that I thought citizens should be thinking about.

In reflection, what were the lessons from this last run that other candidates can learn from?

(1)   Come in with your own ideas and concerns. Think about what you would like to see the City do better, what new challenges need to be faced, and what your vision is for your community.

(2)   Fundraise. You need money to run a political race. Although only $20,000 was spent on my 2024 campaign, other leading candidates spent between $200,000 and $275,000. Start early to put your finances in good shape so once the race begins, you can focus on your message instead of the fundraising.

(3)   A municipal race is almost always about the same issues. People care about taxes, safety and security, transportation (potholes, snow removal) and housing affordability.

(4) The media often have candidate favourites. Some attempt to hide their bias, others don't. Be prepared for not being anyone's favourite.

(5) Tell the truth – you may not win but you can look at yourself in the mirror at the end of the day. If you made promises during your campaign that you knew could not be accomplished or fulfilled and you win, you are now in the uncomfortable position of backpedalling or changing your public stance. Either way, you are not authentic.

Throughout my time as mayor, I had a small plaque on my desk. Before that I carried it with me to council meetings and kept it in front me throughout our deliberations. It was the Rotary 4-Way Test. It read:

(1) Is it the TRUTH?
(2) Is it FAIR to all concerned?
(3) Will it build GOOD WILL and BETTER FRIENDSHIPS?
(4) Will it be BENEFICIAL to all concerned?

If you are contemplating running for any public office, you need to commit to that 4-Way Test. To do anything less, you will fail in your responsibility to your community, to your family, and to yourself.

Being on a city council is like living in a glass house. For those on the outside looking in, it is always easier to be critical, even malicious, than to actually step up and volunteer to make things better. That's why people who enter politics generally have very genuine respect for other elected public leaders, even those with whom they very strongly disagree.

For example, former City Councillor Lenore Swysten and I have had very different ideas about how to improve our city, and she's been very critical of me at times, but I will always applaud her willingness to put her name and her ideals on the line. I have much less time for the constant complainers who seek publicity by being controversial and counter-productive, but who have never come up with one good idea to better their community, ever. It's easy to complain or say something isn't right, but what is your solution?

If you are one of those few who would even consider running for public office, thank you. Democracies work only through participation, through intelligent and respectful debate and, ultimately, in choice – our right to vote, which is what we should cherish far more than we do.

Make sure you run for the right reasons. It's a mistake to decide to run just because of one issue, regardless of how passionate you are about it. Don't aspire to be a city councillor just so you can improve the park in your neighbourhood, or fix the potholes on your particular street, or because you carry a grudge against a particular department at City Hall.

I also think it is a mistake for anyone to run for mayor without first serving on your city council. First of all, it immediately tells me you really do not understand how civic government works and suggests that you're more in love with the idea of being mayor – of the profile you'll have and how good it will look on your resume – than you are in doing the long hard work of being mayor.

Running for mayor in a city the size of Saskatoon represents a significant financial risk, because you're campaigning across the entire city. Far better to run in your own ward, where you should have already built up a reputation for honesty, love of your community, and an ability to listen to and work with others.

Even before you decide to run for City Council, you might want to expand your experience with civic government through one of the more than 20 boards and committees that you can apply to sit on. I guarantee you'll find something that will appeal to your particular interests. Are you an ardent dog or cat lover? The Advisory Committee on Animal Control has to have five members of the general public. What qualifications do you need? "This committee is open to any adult resident of Saskatoon with an interest in pets and pet control." You meet once a month, the fourth Thursday. Or are you interested in community planning and development? The Municipal Planning Commission requires "ten people who are not

City of Saskatoon employees," with the only stipulation that you not be there to "represent a particular interest group." The commission meets at noon on the fourth Tuesday of the month.

Being on a municipal board or commission is a great way to get to know at least one city councillor better, as well as other influential people in the city. It gives you a sampling of how civic government works, and good practice at presenting your point of view to others who may see things quite differently. However, if those monthly time commitments seem too onerous, trust me, you do not want to be a member of the city council of a large municipality.

I like to think of city councillors and the mayor much more as community volunteers than politicians. Federal or provincial politics do not belong in council chambers. If you want to be an advocate for the Saskatchewan Party, the NDP, the Green Party, the Conservatives, or the Liberals, then good for you. Go for it, and enjoy the fierce debates that await you! Just make sure you sign up to play in the right league, and it isn't civic government. In civic government, you should be willing, and unfettered, to make the best decision for the most people – to be able to change your mind on any issue, after careful decision, without having to "cross the floor." I would tell new councillors that they should come to every meeting with "a mind open to persuasion."

One of the first things I tell anyone who asks me about running for City Council is, "Go home and have a good long talk with your partner, your family, with anyone who is going to be affected by what will be a major change in your life." What will it be like for your spouse to go to work or a community event and hear stinging criticism of his or her partner? How will the family feel about you missing birthday parties and other celebrations?

I was very lucky to have a very forgiving family, because over my term as mayor I managed to miss at least one of each of my kids' birthdays. I would come home late in the evening to find a piece of birthday cake on a plate, covered with plastic wrap. For any parent, it's not the best feeling in the world, I can tell you that. I don't think it's any surprise that none of my kids were interested in taking over the store, because they saw what it took, and the toll on the home front. For the same reason, they have shown no interest in running for public office of any kind.

Being a mayor means you're on call, at all times. Regardless of where I was, including my brief weeks of vacation, I always left my itinerary with the staff along with ways to reach me. I don't drink alcohol, just as a personal choice. I have wondered, though, about mayors who do. What happens if you get a call at 3 a.m., and you're still feeling the effects of that birthday or anniversary you just celebrated? How could you make decisions in that state, in an emergency?

Regardless of what you might think of his conduct during the Trump era, Rudy Giuliani was without question a great mayor of New York City. He followed that Boy

Scouts motto, "Be prepared." Even though nobody could have ever imagined what happened on 9/11, Giuliani's insistence on being always ready for the unexpected was tremendously valuable when disaster hit his city.

Thank goodness I never had anything close to that level of crisis during my term as mayor. The two worst incidents were both weather-related, perhaps not surprisingly. The first was in January 2007, when the city was hit with one of the worst snowstorms in our history. It started in the early afternoon, and by 3 p.m., people were trying to get home as fast as they could, to be with their families before the worst of the storm began. I stayed at the office until eight that night, until I was sure everything that needed to be done had been done, including my going on television to reassure everyone that things would be alright. I remember being asked if we should shut down transit services the next morning. I refused, because I wanted as much normalcy as possible. "We're not going to be like Toronto and call in the army," I remember saying. As it turned out, things did get back to normal, surprisingly quickly. That's my Saskatoon!

The other weather crisis happened the same day I was scheduled to fly to Ottawa to attend a garden party for Queen Elizabeth. That evening, we had a record downpour over a very short period of time. I was in the taxi on the way to the airport, and the driver told me of how some streets in the west end were impassable. I immediately told him to take me to one of the sites, the corner of Diefenbaker and Centennial Drive. Once I saw the flooding and talked to some of our workers on the site, I had the taxi driver take me back to the airport so I could cancel my flight, then went straight downtown to get to work. If it's any consolation to my wife and children, it wasn't just them who I stood up on a special occasion because of my job – I even cancelled my date with the Queen.

Yes, the support and understanding of your family is essential, especially during the highly stressful times. I can never say enough about the importance of good friends, too, and during your time in politics you will most certainly find out who your true friends are! After a day where you've been misquoted in the media, or taken some calls from angry taxpayers, or been portrayed as some kind of tyrant by a special interest group, it is so good to have someone give you a pat on the back. To good friends everywhere, and to every citizen, please make our city stronger and your representatives even better by taking the time once in awhile to acknowledge good work and good decisions through a phone call or personal note. You have no idea how much that can mean some days.

One of my saddest times was the passing of a friend and colleague, Councillor Moe Neault. It was after one of the most contentious committee meetings during my entire time as councillor and mayor. The issue under discussion was recycling and whether or not the contract

Everyone deserves peace, prosperity, and freedom.

for recycling should go to the incumbent partner, Cosmopolitan Industries, or to a private company.

I had been to Cosmo's operations many times, including their Christmas parties. I greatly admired what Howie Stensrud, Al Anderson, and his colleagues had done for Saskatoon, and I admired the great people at Cosmo who found meaningful employment despite their intellectual challenges. Cosmopolitan Industries also understood the intricacies of recycling and had serious doubts about the proposal to take recycling out of their hands. (I shared their views, and as it turns out, they were right in their predictions.)

After that heated meeting, I went home, very disappointed that the executive committee decided to reject the Cosmo proposal. Late that night, I was still quietly fuming over the whole episode when I got the call. Moe had suffered a heart attack and passed away. I have often wondered how much the turmoil of that meeting was a contributing factor. It's when you're feeling that low that you realize how important your partner, family, and friends can be to you.

The other person you should talk to before running for office is your employer, your staff, or your business partner. If you're truly fulfilling your duties on City Council, your performance at work is going to suffer. There's no way around it. You cannot give 100 per cent to two things at once. Take the time to talk to a current or former city councillor, and get a good idea of what time commitment you will have to make, then make sure you come to a clear understanding with co-workers or partners. It's far better to address potential issues before they arise. I sincerely hope everyone will be supportive of what you're doing and the personal sacrifices you might be making, in terms of salary and promotion, in order to serve your city.

Let's suppose you've got the backing of family, friends, and your employer or work colleagues. The next consideration is the cost of time and money. As I said before, running to be a councillor on your ward is far more realistic for most citizens than throwing your hat in for the mayor's job.

Think of it this way. There are thirteen constituencies in Saskatoon for MLAs, and three ridings for MPs; when you're running for mayor, you're running in all of those jurisdictions combined! In my 2020 election campaign, I was fortunate to have more than a hundred volunteers. As for costs, in that election, I and my principal opponent, Charlie Clark, each reported more than $200,000 in campaign contributions. Compare that to the contributions to the campaigns of the successful candidates for City Council, which came in at roughly $15,000 to $20,000, or ten per cent of the campaigns for mayor.

If you have everything in place, congratulations! You're ready to run for public office – except for one more thing, the most important thing: vision. Great communities were built by people who were able to think big, and when disaster struck, were not overwhelmed by what was in front of them, who could see past the here and now. Yes, you will be criticized. You might even be called Canada's craziest mayor some day. Or worse.

If people laughed at me for having pipe dreams during my time as councillor and mayor, I in turn was always frustrated by those who had no dreams at all. How disappointing that we couldn't get six votes to replace the Traffic Bridge with something modern, the result of a design competition. How sad to hear the critics who see the world only in black and white, and always as either-or. Why the argument over fixing the streets versus building a world-class art gallery? Why can we not find ways to do both?

Your greatest challenge – and the true test of your ability to be a councillor or mayor – will be to find ways to get things done. I remember the day when business leader Greg Yuel came to visit me and said, "We need a new football field."

I told him he was absolutely right, but he was not getting it from the City. I could tell he was ready to explode. "But before you go off," I continued, "I'll tell you how you are going to get it. You're going to go before Council and say that you're going to raise half, but the other half will need to come from City Council. They will then feel much more like they need to live up to their end of the bargain and will proceed." Look at what we have at the Gordie Howe Sports Complex now. The city invested $4 million, but fundraising hit close to $20 million. Is that not a good deal for the city?

There are countless examples of our great city's resolve to do things people say we have no business doing – of being far more than anybody thought we could be, simply because we were not afraid to say, "Yes we can!"

When I look at Saskatoon, I see possibilities waiting to be realized, opportunities to be taken, people who can come together in the spirit of extraordinary hope and confidence.

Who wouldn't want to play a role in that?

Acknowledgements

I would first like to thank all those who volunteered during my years in civic politics — without you the city would not be what it is today. Thank you for your belief in me, asking for nothing in return other than for me to work hard, be honest, and make the city feel good about itself. To all the voters who voted for me, believing your vote could and would will make a difference — thank you. It was an honour to represent each and every citizen of Saskatoon.

Thank you to Carol Purich and City Solicitor Theresa Dust for being such stalwarts, making sure we kept the Office of the Mayor beyond reproach, even though there were those who tried so desperately to work against that goal. I will never forget the comment, "Before you do anything, think about how your family would feel if they read about it on the front page of the newspaper."

There are so many people who helped in shaping who I am today. I'm sure I will miss mentioning some of you, but know that this is not unintentional. Thank you —

To my teachers who always expected me to give it my best and pushed me to a height many may not have thought possible.

To my hockey coaches who volunteered, not because they had a child of their own on the team, but to give boys a chance to do something positive.

To my football coaches who demanded nothing less than perfection: my junior coach, Mr. Wallace and my senior coaches, Mr. Regush, Mr. Earl, and Mr. Balon. You helped shape my views in life. "Success is a team effort, no one can reach it by themselves. It takes a team working in sync."

To Malcolm Stalk, who believed in me and my teammates when no one else thought we could not only not win a game but go on to become Provincial Champions and Canada Game representatives.

To Jack McLeod (Coach and G.M. of the Blades) for giving me the chance to play in the Western Hockey League, creating the opportunity for me to be drafted into the NHL.

To Coach Marc Boileau (of the farm teams for the Pittsburgh Penguins farm teams) who demanded I learn the game and understand life in general.

To the Brodsky family (owners of the Blades) for giving me the opportunity to work with young, hopeful hockey players who wanted to fulfil their dreams of playing in the NHL.

Thank you to all the customers who shopped at Atch & Co. over the years. You taught me the value of having great relationships with those you know and how much those relationships can mean.

Thank you to the Masons and Shriners, who I have been pleased to be a member of for many years. Thank you for wanting to help the children in our communities to have a better quality of life.

Thank you to those on council for all their different points of view and for their willingness to work together for the good of the city. I must particularly mention Councillor Myles Heidt who was an absolute stalwart in getting the different projects across the goal line. We may not always have agreed on everything but we both wanted what was best for the city. Also to Councillor Langford (who gave me a compliment I have never forgotten - that I was the conscience of council) and to Councillor Lorje (for saying I had done more for the city's west side than any other mayor, which was a kind comment).

Thank you to Chief Bear who I worked so closely with over the years on many projects, including the placing of the John Lake and Chief Whitecap statues along with the War of 1812 "Spirit of Alliance."

Thank you to the Muskeg Lake Reserve for the positive interactions we have had over the years.

Thank you to Saskatoon's faith-based community. Congratulations in having the second largest prayer breakfast in all of North America.

Thank you to the Rawlco media stations, Saskatoon Media Group, CTV, and Global. You were all great in wanting to get out a positive message of the city.

Since leaving politics — I would like to thank those

who have given me the opportunity to work with them, bringing different ideas forward. For this, I am so grateful.

To those who read this book — I hope I leave you with a better understanding of what it takes to be a local politician and what to expect. Thank you for reading *Building Bridges*.

About the Author

Donald James Atchison was Mayor of Saskatoon (the largest city in the province of Saskatchewan) from 2003 to 2016. Atchison was elected mayor four times. When he lost his bid for a fifth term in 2016, he left office as the longest-serving mayor in the city's history at 13 years. Atchison oversaw a period of rapid economic growth, emphasizing the development of new neighbourhoods, infrastructure, and the renewal of the River Landing development adjacent to downtown. He was re-elected by wide margins in 2006 and 2009, before earning a narrow bid for a fourth term in 2012. As term limits for Saskatchewan municipal councils were extended at this time to four years, Atchison's fourth term made make him the longest serving mayor in the city's history.

Atchison was born and raised in Saskatoon, Saskatchewan. He was a standout ice hockey goaltender from an early age, and he played junior hockey for the Saskatoon Blades in the 1971–72 season. In 1972, Atchison was drafted by the NHL's Pittsburgh Penguins. Although he did not ultimately play in the NHL, Atchison had a brief professional career in the United States before returning to Saskatoon and joining the family business, the men's wear store Atch & Co. He was offered a role in the 1977 hockey film, Slap Shot, but turned the opportunity down, thinking it was a joke.

Atchison was first elected to Saskatoon's city council in 1994 as councillor for the newly created Ward 10, and was re-elected in 1997 and acclaimed in 2000. He was well known for his campaigning style of standing on street corners and waving at passing motorists, a tactic that was eventually outlawed. Atchison was first elected as mayor on October 22, 2003, running on a platform that included being tough on crime, freezing property taxes, centralizing control of city management, and resuming control of the city's police commission.

In 2016, Atchison launched a bid for what would have been a record-setting fifth term as mayor. He was ultimately defeated by former City Councillor Charlie Clark.

Atchison and his wife, Mardele, have five children and thirteen grandchildren.

www.ingramcontent.com/pod-product-compliance
Lightning Source LLC
Chambersburg PA
CBHW060227030426
42335CB00014B/1363